WHO WILL TEACH
FOR AMERICA?

ALSO BY MICHAEL SHAPIRO

Japan: In the Land of the Brokenhearted
The Shadow in the Sun: A Korean Year of Love and Sorrow

WHO WILL TEACH
FOR AMERICA?

by

Michael Shapiro

FARRAGUT PUBLISHING COMPANY
WASHINGTON, D.C.

PRINTED IN THE UNITED STATES OF AMERICA.
Design by Donald Corren
Production by Thatcher Drew
First printing 1993

Library of Congress Cataloging-in-Publication Data

Shapiro, Michael, 1952-
    Who will Teach for America? / by Michael Shapiro.
        p.   cm.
    Includes bibliographical references
    ISBN 0-918535-18-2
    1. First year teachers – United States – Case studies.
2. Teach for America (Project) 3. Teachers – United States –
Attitudes. 4. Education. Urban – United States – Case Studies.
I. Title.
LB2844. 1.N4S53 1993
371. 1'00973–dc20   93-4905 CIP

In Memory of Harry Ackerman

Contents

Introduction

This is how they look at you: With empty eyes, angry eyes, knowing eyes and eyes that seek understanding that eludes them. They are saying many things at once, much of it contradictory. They are saying I want to learn and I don't want to learn, tell me to sit down and don't dare tell me to sit down, I want you to like me and I hate you. They say I want to try and I am afraid to try because if I try and fail I will just confirm what I already know. They are saying that school matters and school cannot matter because if I say it matters then I am a chump, a wannabe, a fool. If I want to learn you cannot know it.

They are sitting in rows, or in groups of four or five clustered around tables. They are looking at you, the teacher, waiting to fail, waiting for you to fail, sometimes doing their best to make sure you fail, hoping you won't.

Maybe they know you went to Harvard, or Yale, or Stanford or the University of Michigan and maybe they know what that means: that early on you discovered that you liked school and were good at school, so good that you could go on to one of the colleges that so many want to go to. The odds do not favor their following you. They are yours for forty-five minutes a day, or from eight to three. You want them to leave you seeing school as you saw it. You will spend a lot of time wondering whether you are making any difference at all.

Nothing you have done, no class you've taken, no course load you've endured, no job you've worked is as hard as teaching these children. You ask yourself, Why am I doing this and when can I quit?

In the spring of 1988, a Princeton senior named Wendy Kopp sat at a conference listening to people lament the sorry shape of American education. As she listened, an idea began taking shape, one that would be the basis for her senior thesis. In that thesis she outlined a plan in which a corps of graduates from the nation's best universities would commit to teach for two years in some of the nation's most troubled schools.

Her adviser, Marvin Bressler, was as dubious as he was protective. He did not want to see her get hurt: "Any sane human being who felt the slightest degree of responsibility for her would have told her, as I did: 'Kid, you're deranged.'"

Kopp did not agree. With a degree of pragmatism and sense for business acumen that would leave interviewers nonplused — "Where's the youthful passion? Where's the innocent idealism?" — Kopp secured $26,000 in seed money from the Mobil Corporation, and donated office space from Union Carbide. And Teach for America was born.

Wendy Kopp is one of those people who regards doubts as so many flies to be swatted away. She was going to raise money to start her program and get important corporate names to put on Teach for America's letterhead. She was going to use those names to raise still more money and form a group of corporate sponsors. By the time she went back to Mobil for more funding, she explained that the minimum donation for sponsors had climbed to $100,000. Mobil paid.

Then she set about finding her teachers. She dispatched 100 campus representatives on a national recruiting drive. They hung posters in college libraries and stuffed flyers in seniors' mailboxes. Then Kopp and her young staff waited. And what they soon discovered was that they had tapped a vein far richer than most anyone thought. From a generation dismissed for its self-absorption came 2,500 applications for the first 500 spots in Teach for America.

*   *   *

News of Kopp's campaign spread quickly. Stories about her and Teach for America ran on front pages across the country. The program was featured on television news shows, and lauded on the editorial pages. The story was, journalistically, a natural: Here, in the midst of all the dark and sorry news about American education came an intriguing idea from a very unlikely source. What could be better than bringing into the nation's classrooms a corps of college graduates who, in all likelihood, would have never considered careers in education? And not just any classrooms, but ones that most teachers hurried to leave, where rookie teachers proceeded at their peril; classrooms that were the symbol of the decline of American education.

And Kopp was not talking about getting them there in a year or two or five. She was not talking like someone who needed the input of a lot of consultants who would tell her why her plan could not work. She was talking about getting teachers into classrooms for the coming school year. If there was a certain beauty to the plan it was its simplicity. Smart kids in poor schools: A Peace Corps for Teachers.

Kopp had reasoned that one of the ways to make the program attractive was to make it competitive. In addition to an interview, applicants had to submit an essay and teach a sample lesson. Kopp wanted people who were not only bright and enthusiastic but who also displayed the capacity for flexibility and adaptability. "People have to be prepared for an English teaching position and then teach math," she said. "We're recruiting a pool of teachers who are excited about teaching where they're teaching."

She was also selecting people who stood in sharp contrast to most of their contemporaries entering the field. The women's movement had expanded career opportunities for millions of women who might once have been left with few choices other than teaching and nursing. This meant that a vast pool of potential teaching talent had been drained. Today the sad fact is that most graduates of schools of education are not the best students. They graduate high school not with A's but with average grades of C+ to B-, marks that place them, on the average, in the 70th percentile of their classes. They enter college with Scholastic Aptitude Test scores of 950 out of a possible 1600. Teach for America, on the other hand, boasted a corps of teachers who had averaged 1251 on the SATs. In its first two years, the program would attract 41 graduates from Yale, 31 from Cornell, 23 from Georgetown, 22 from Stanford and 21 from Harvard. And unlike the overwhelming majority of new teachers who are white — as opposed to 4.7 percent who are African-American, 1.6 percent who are Latino, and 1.5 percent who are Asian-America — Teach for America reported that in its first two corps of teachers, virtually a quarter were from minority groups.

Kopp and her staff culled through the applications and selected their 500. They brought them to California, to the campus of the University of Southern California in the summer of 1989. And there is set about trying to teach them to be teachers. They had eight weeks.

The fledging teachers learned the basic lessons of educational theory and practice, as taught by teacher educators. The lectures were augmented with student teaching in the Los Angeles public schools. Later, much would be made of that training, especially by the corps members themselves who would complain that for all the talk of theory, they were left unprepared for what to expect in the classroom.

But that first week, filled with youthful passion and inspiring talk, the reality of what awaited them seemed very far away. Still, there were those who knew something about what was to come and who offered warnings. At one inspirational gathering, the speaker asked all the corps members to rise and turn to the person next to them, offer a hand and say, "I am a teacher."

Among the corps members sat Tom Rinaldi, who had taught in Pittsburgh. Rinaldi turned, stuck out his hand and greeted his neighbor.

"I am a teacher," he said.

"I am a teacher," said his eager new friend.

"No," said Rinaldi who, assuming the role of Jeremiah, added, "I am a teacher."

But that was in the summer, before the teaching began. In the course of those frenzied weeks at USC the perils of the classroom were eclipsed by a sense of mission. Wendy Kopp was not just talking about finding new teachers. She was talking about the changes those teachers might bring to a system in desperate need of reform. "Everyone's saying our schools are bad, or that they're the same as they were 100 or 200 years ago," Kopp later said. "Our world is so different. Our families are so different. Our workplaces are different. And our schools are not."

Kopp, who'd grown up in Dallas attending public schools, and whose parents ran a guidebook company, did not invent Teach for America unaware of the way things got done. As an undergraduate she worked for the Foundation for Student Communication, a Princeton organization that not only establishes links with business leaders and holds an annual conference between those leaders and students, but also publishes one of the largest student-run magazines in the country. When Kopp was a freshman the foundation's annual budget was $300,000. By her senior year, when she was president, it was $1.5 million. "Everything I do is based on that experience," she told The New York Times in 1989. "It taught me a lot about how to strategize and how to manage people. I realized that there's an incredible amount of money in the world and people who are looking for good things to support, and if you just get in the door you can have a good chance of making it fly."

That it did. Yet with all the acclaim that greeted its birth, Teach for America also drew sharp criticism. It came primarily from teacher educators who charged that the very premise on which Teach for America was founded — find smart people, train them quickly and get them into difficult classrooms — only undermined a profession whose standing was already low. The critics charged that Teach for America was created on the mistaken belief that teaching was so easily mastered a job that anyone with a degree from a good university could learn to do it in eight weeks.

The critics also charged that Teach for America was doing nothing short of using the nation's most disadvantaged children — the children who most needed the best teaching — as guinea pigs for training a band of well-intended but unprepared teachers.

*   *   *

The fanfare that greeted Teach for America helped place at the center of the debate about education reform the very people upon whom success and failure in school rested: teachers.

There are 2.3 million teachers in America. Women outnumber men by a ratio of nearly four to one. The median age of teachers is forty-one, the annual average salary is $24,000, and length of service fifteen years. When the Metropolitan Life Insurance Company asked teachers in 1986 how many thought of leaving the profession, 55 percent of those surveyed said they had. And when the Department of Education asked teachers whether they would choose their same career path if given a second chance, 20 percent said they were only halfway sure they would, 22 percent said they probably wouldn't and just over 9 percent said they definitely would not. When asked about their satisfaction with their jobs, half of all the teachers surveyed said they were considering going into another field; just over one in five said they would probably leave the field in the next five years.

Teachers are underpaid, overburdened and feel themselves to be unappreciated — by students, parents and administrators. Time and again teachers speak about being left out of any meaningful discussion about their schools. The result is often a feeling of powerlessness. But unlike their contemporaries who'd endured four years of education school seeing themselves and their careers as second-best, Teach for America's corps members were the kind of college graduates who enjoyed that wonderful youthful belief in themselves. They were like the eager suitor who despite admonitions about falling in love with a heartbreaker still believes that he will be different. These teachers came into schools whose sorry reputations preceded them, believing that because of who they were and what they'd done, they could make a difference.

Then the doors closed behind them and they were left alone with a classroom of students who knew only that before them stood a new teacher who had not yet shown any reason why they should bother listening.

*   *   *

Wendy Kopp had, intentionally or not, stumbled onto something far larger than a teacher placement service. She had issued not only a call to service, but a challenge — to her generation, to the educational establishment, and to a nation that has for too long dismissed the people who teach its children as second-best professionals. Had the nation's schools been stocked with well-prepared teachers, and had the schools of education been turning away marvelous applicants, Teach for America would have had no reason to exist. That it did offered stark evidence of the void that existed in the American classroom.

But had Kopp found a new and better way to enlist, train and place teachers? And could those teachers infuse new life into America's most moribund classrooms? Or did the obstacles that had overwhelmed so many other teachers prove just as overwhelming to Wendy Kopp's corps? What happened when Teach for America's well-educated and well-intended teachers went back to school? What did they learn about teaching? What did they learn about themselves?

There were lessons to be learned in the stories of that group of teachers — lessons about what it will take to make schools a place where most everyone can learn, and lessons about what it means to be a teacher.

In the course of their education Teach for America's teachers would begin to learn that to be a good teacher means knowing not only the subject, but the difference between a violent child who is begging for attention, and the child who is filled with uncontrollable rage. They would learn that control does not mean keeping children in their seats, but keeping them engaged and excited.

They would encounter the maze of obstacles that stand in way of teaching: bureaucracies that impose outdated and arbitrary curriculum guidelines that do little to enhance real learning; neighborhoods where children come of age surrounded by poverty, drug addiction, broken families, disease and death.

They would learn how much there was more to know than could be learned in a single year of teaching — let alone after eight weeks of training. They would learn just what it takes to become a teacher.

But there would be something more, and that would be a lesson about hope. These teachers would learn that there are people in America's classrooms who want to teach, who are searching for ways to connect to their students. They would learn, too, that there are reformers who are devising new ways to teach, and discovering new ways that learning happens. And, most importantly, they would learn that even among their most difficult students there was still a desire to know and to learn.

*   *   *

This is the story of seven teachers whom Teach for America brought back into the classrooms. It is the story of Ho Choong Chang, a Korean-American from Yale trying to make his junior high school students work at school as relentlessly as he did. It is about Jill Gaulding, an MIT-trained scientist struggling to make her biology students see the beauty and excitement in science.

It is about Miguel Ceballos and Jane Martinez, each of whom return to their old neighborhoods and confront the troubled worlds they left behind. It is about Tom Super, who would not quit after he was fired from his first job and who learned how to take control of a classroom, and about Vicki McGhee working to make her students understand the power of their words. And it is about Julie Burstein who, in the midst of the Los Angeles riots, understands just how great a gulf exists between her world and the world of her students.

If the circumstances of their lives sound familiar, that is intentional. This book is an outgrowth of the Emmy-nominated PBS documentary of the same title. It picks up where the documentary left off, exploring the lives and experiences of seven of the same teachers featured in the film.

There were days when these fledgling teachers went home in tears and days when they wanted to quit. And then there were days when they looked out at their students, caught their eyes, asked a question and saw a hand raised. And then another hand, and then another.

1

What's Passing?

Ho Choong Chang (Yale, '90)

NEVER ASK MR. CHANG "WHAT'S PASSING?" He'll take your head off. He'll give you the speech. Everyone in Mr. Chang's seventh grade earth science classes knows the speech because every time he hands back a test or quiz, someone asks, "Mr. Chang, What's passing?"

Then Mr. Chang begins. He says, "Do not ask 'what is passing?' That is an insult to you. It says to me 'I did not study enough.' If you studied you would know you passed. It is an insult to me."

Passing, in Mr. Chang's view, is not a goal. Excellence is a goal. He's hung slogans on the closet: "Hard Work. Optimism. Perseverance. Energy," and over the blackboard, "The Pursuit of Excellence." These are not just words for Mr. Chang. He believes in them and wants his students to believe in them, too. But he cannot seem to make the students see them as anything more than boldly printed words that, at first viewing, might bring a nod and a "yeah" — as in "Excellence. Cool" — and, subsequently, something to stare at when the mind wanders. It is Mr. Chang's second year of teaching, second year of trying to find a way to instill in his 100 students the idea of seeing school a new way, the way he saw it — as a place where succeeding is not merely getting by.

But no matter how hard he tries, no matter how many times he delivers his speech, no matter how often he talks to parents, his students seek his reassurance that the passing grade is still seventy-five. Ten points above the standard at most schools, seventy-five is the passing grade for all classes in Satellite East Junior High School, in the Brooklyn neighborhood of Bedford-Stuyvesant. You have to want to go to Satellite East, or at least your parents have to want you to go there. Admission is selective, except for those who live in the catchment area and who in the course of the year get bounced out of other schools and into Satellite East. But even if you punched a teacher in your old school you are expected to pass with seventy-fives in Satellite East. That is unless you're in Mr. Chang's class, where you are never to ask, "What's passing?"

This year, on the first day of school, Mr. Chang was ready. When someone asked the question he shot back, "Why are you concerned with passing?"

"Because," replied the questioner, "I don't want to fail."

"Why don't you want to fail?" asked Mr. Chang.

"I don't know."

"Don't you know? Don't you know that you will study hard and pass all your tests?"

A lot of kids don't pass Mr. Chang's tests. They don't do their homework, or if they do, they don't have their parents sign the homework, as the school requests. Students regularly come late because, they tell him, they do not like school and therefore see no reason not to sleep a half hour more. When he asks why they do not have their homework the diligent ones among them tell him of after-school jobs; others say that evenings are devoted to television and Nintendo. He tells them that all he is asking is for twenty minutes between 3 P.M. and 11 P.M. Mr. Chang has given up on lectures about television because no one listened.

Mr. Chang's students are clever, just as students in most every school in every city in every state in the union are clever. If they learn nothing else in school they learn a lesson that can last a lifetime: what is the least that is expected of me. Even if Mr. Chang raises the stakes they have nonetheless branded into their minds the essential number 75.

In his bearing, in his speech — clipped, precise, devoid of contractions — in the rapid, demanding way in which he conducts the give and take of his class, Mr. Chang embodies the discipline he longs to instill. Yet he remains a pedagogical Sisyphus: demanding excellence, scheduling a test, arranging for extra tutoring, hectoring his students to come prepared, only to be asked, once again, the minimum requirement. "I like to have an edge in every situation," he says, confounded. "Here I don't have an edge."

For in their inevitable question, comes another equally discomfiting question that Mr. Chang asks himself: Am I passing?

*   *   *

Ho Choong Chang grew up in Coopersburg, a suburb of Allentown, Pennsylvania. He was born in Malaysia, en route from Korea to the United States. His father, a master in the Korean martial art of taekwondo, first taught judo at Lehigh University and later opened his own taekwondo academy. Ho and his two younger brothers spent every afternoon after school and every Saturday morning at the academy, at the knee of their father, who rather than make allowances for his sons, only made their training more rigorous. Once, an old girlfriend, after meeting his father, told Ho, "he has eyes that can pierce my soul." Ho, thinking of his unnerving calm and self-possessed father, did not disagree.

Taekwondo, like all martial arts, is not simply a means of combat. Its early practitioners were a band of scholar-warriors, intent on creating the perfect man by developing the spirit as well as the body. Taekwondo is rooted in the seemingly contradictory premise that while perfection is unattainable, it is nonetheless the only true goal. The world of taekwondo is a simple place. Kicks and blows are delivered only one way, the right way, the way the master does it. The master is never wrong. Elders are always wiser. Students, no matter how proficient, can never surpass their masters or their elders. In the taekwondo academy, and in the home in which Ho Chang grew up, life proceeds along clear and immutable lines.

The one choice Ho was given as a child was his name. His parents offered him the option of keeping his Korean name, or choosing a new, American one. After considering Christian, Christopher and Dexter, he chose to keep the name his parents had given him. "It would have been almost an insult to change it," he says. There were no other significant choices to make because his parents made the choices for him. His father told him, "After you turn 21 you may start thinking on your own."

Ho was to be a doctor. Later this was amended with a specialty, plastic surgery, which his father heard was highly profitable. Ho was going to Harvard. Not Yale. Harvard. Ho listened to his teachers and if he did not like a certain teacher he listened anyway. He was the student and did as he was told. After school came homework and after homework taekwondo. Television was a privilege granted on Saturday afternoons. Ho had little sense of the lives of his friends. He knew that his parents were more rigid than their parents, that he got better grades and that on Saturday afternoons his friends got to go to the movies. On Saturday afternoons, after taekwondo, Ho and his brothers shot baskets at the hoop their father had hung for them and watched kung-fu movies on the television. By the time he was eighteen, Ho had been to the movies exactly ten times. On Sundays the family went to church.

Because his father worked long hours discipline was left primarily to Ho's mother who, as is common in Korean households, did not shy away from using the belt. Still, on report card day Ho and his brothers faced their father. Report card day was also allowance day. For each A the boys got they received five dollars. For every B their father smacked them on the back of the calves with a bamboo pole. The pole, used on less than capable taekwondo students, raised a nasty welt. In the Chang home Cs, Ds and Fs, "were not even discussed" and jeans and sneakers were not dispensed, but "earned" through As.

None of this, in a Korean context, was unusual. In fact, it displayed far more concern and involvement with school than most Korean fathers have time to give. The children are the mother's work, and where school is concerned she can be expected to lean on them, badger them about grades and homework, especially in the senior year of high school. That is the time for college entrance exams, and it is often said in Korea that the student who sleeps four hours a night passes, but the one who sleeps five fails. Failure means not getting into the school of your choice, which means not being on the track for the job of your parents' choice. In Korea, as in Japan, there is no path to success other than school. So mothers, and sometimes fathers, will be waiting for their weary teenagers when they come home, late at night, from study hall. They will have coffee ready and if their children doze, they will be outside the door, knocking, reminding them that they are not yet done. Ho's mother and father were not being cruel. They were honoring their responsibility as parents, just as Ho and his equally diligent brothers were honoring theirs as devoted children.

At Southern Lehigh High School Ho was news editor of the school paper, index editor and head typist of the school yearbook, winner of the Junior Achievement "President of the Year" award, vice president of the National Honor Society chapter, vice president of the ecology club, and a member of the tennis and quiz bowl teams. Out of class of 225 students, he graduated fifth, "much," he says, "to the chagrin of my parents."

By the spring of his senior year, having done as was expected of him, he joined students all over the country in waiting to hear which colleges wanted him. So it was one afternoon, that his mother — having waited until tennis practice was over — appeared outside of school, bearing three envelopes. The ones from Penn and Yale were thick. Harvard's was not. Ignoring the obvious acceptances, he tore open the rejection from Harvard and ran into the school building, crying.

That night, after his mother insisted that he open the acceptance letters from Yale and Penn — which chose him as one of only 50 students for a distinguished scholarship — Ho's father came to his room. It was eleven o'clock and Ho had spent most of the evening in the bathroom, sobbing. He tried to clean his face before facing his father, who had once punished him by making him stand for three hours with his nose pressed against a wall. But his father was not angry now. Instead he said, "You know that we wanted you to go to Harvard. Perhaps we pushed you too hard."

Only two other times would his father be so accepting of a goal unachieved. The first was when Ho narrowly missed making the United States Olympic Taekwondo Team. The second was when he announced that he was delaying his application to medical school to teach in Brooklyn. But by then Ho was twenty-one years and three months old, and according to their pact, his father, though disapproving, would not stand in his way.

*   *   *

"Let's say you did not do your best," says Mr. Chang. "Let's say you got a sixty out of 100. Obviously you will be disappointed."

It is the first period after lunch and Mr. Chang allows only minimal bustling and chit-chat before class. Today is the day for presenting the results of experiments the students have conducted at home. But first Mr. Chang has a proposal: Those wishing to better their grades on the exam he is returning can take the test again. They can study over the upcoming holidays. The new grade will be the average of the first and second scores, with the second score counted twice. Students can take the test as many times as they like, with the prospect of improving their scores each time.

Everyone in Mr. Chang's classes knows just how well everyone else is doing because Mr. Chang not only posts every grade for every test, but calculates each student's percentile ranking in class. Borrowing on a practice of Asian schools, Mr. Chang believes that if you are going to be a screw-up in his class, you will pay the price in a bit of public humiliation.

"Who does not want to go today?" he asks. A hand shoots up. Mr. Chang says, "You are first."

The class applauds Charles' presentation and neatly printed poster-board display of his experiment on bio-degradability. But Mr. Chang does not want any applause until the questions end. The class is allowed three questions and then Mr. Chang asks his. At the end of class Mr. Chang will say, "I was very nice today. The questions today were easy." He is fooling no one.

He asks Charles how he conducted his experiment, and Charles tells him how he had placed half an apple in a fish tank and each day added a half cup of water. After four weeks all that remained of the apple were the seeds. Apples, Charles concludes, are bio-degradable, which is useful information in a world running out of room to throw its trash. Mr. Chang, unsmiling, makes a note in his marking book as Sakeka begins reporting the results of her experiment on the effect of acid rain on plants.

There are imaginative experiments: Can I save my mother money by determining which grows mold more quickly, white or wheat bread? — and experiments long on fancy lettering and short on science: What is AIDS and how do you get it? At 1:50, as the bell rings, someone asks, "What if you bring in a project late. How many points will you take off?"

"Why do you ask?" Mr. Chang says.

"I just want to know."

Mr. Chang walks to the door and says, "You are excused."

Now comes eighth period, the last class of the day. Eighth period brings more experiment results. And it brings Barry.

Barry vexes Mr. Chang. There is no question of Barry's intelligence, or his curiosity. Barry asks questions all the time. He asks questions in class and after class and during lunch break he seeks out Mr. Chang to ask about phenomena he has observed but which he cannot explain. Mr. Chang is pleased that Barry wants to know, although he has come to believe that Barry does not connect this desire with the need to find out for himself. If he has a question he asks the teacher. And in Mr. Chang's view that is not good enough.

Barry does not ask about passing, because passing is not the issue for him. He scores in the eighties; Mr. Chang is convinced he could score in the nineties. Also, Barry does not always do his homework. Mr. Chang has never spoken to Barry's parents; they do not come to open-school night.

Now it is Barry's turn to tell the class the results of his experiment. He lugs his big poster-board to the front of the room and props it on the desk for everyone to see. The display looks as if it was done five minutes before class.

Even students who took the experimental path of least resistance had at least made a point of putting together handsome displays, if only to try to con Mr. Chang into thinking that they had really invested something of themselves in their projects.

Barry has not bothered. He has scrawled his presentation headings in barely legible crayon and haphazardly taped the sheets of his report to the board. He stands, grinning, before his classmates and Mr. Chang, a tall, skinny boy with eager eyes, and a shirttail pulled out of his pants.

"Is this the best project you could have done?" asks Mr. Chang.

Barry begins to say, "No, but..." when Mr. Chang interrupts and says "Stop there."

Barry settles himself on the desk.

"Stand up," snaps Mr. Chang.

Barry has studied the habits of earthworms. He's hypothesized that they will not only seek moist earth but will also avoid light. At home he took five worms and placed them in a tray of dirt that was watered on one side and dry on the other. The worms sought the moist, dark earth.

As Barry explains what he saw he begins to giggle, composing himself only when Mr. Chang asks impatiently, "How many times did you try the experiment?"

"One time with five worms, all at the same time," says Barry, perhaps aware but seemingly uninterested in the possibility that he might have satisfied his great curiosity by pushing himself to do more than was necessary.

*   *   *

In his freshman year at Yale Ho Chang failed a test for the first time in his life because he did not feel compelled to excel. He did not set out to fail the test, nor did he do what he had always done, which was to study relentlessly. Instead he drank beer and sought the comfort of his new girlfriend.

When he did study, it was in the most cursory way. The test was in general chemistry, a subject he thought he knew well enough to coast. The mean on the test was 51. Ho got a forty-one. Almost as devastating as the grade itself was the look given him by the teaching assistant when he handed back the test. It was, Ho recalls, a look of profound indifference, a look that said, "you are one of the mediocrities."

He did not want to be at Yale. Yale was not Harvard and he had spent twelve years working to get into Harvard. That Yale was Harvard's equal did not matter; the goal was not achieved. So he drifted. Getting out of bed was an effort. He continued his taekwondo training, hoping to make the Olympic team. But without his father, brothers and the academy, he was left to train by himself. He had grown up believing that great effort could overcome limitations. But now he saw only his limitations. He felt very old.

In the spring the academic year, mercifully, ended. And with the burden of his failure, he set off for Korea, to a martial arts college where he would train in earnest.

He was up at five every morning to run five miles. Then he went to the gym, where he was pounded. Koreans, especially college-age Koreans, do not look kindly upon their countrymen who have grown up abroad. Such people, it is said, cannot speak good Korean and do not know Korean ways. They are weak and their parents, who left when the country was still desperately poor, are regarded as traitors. The children are called "bananas," yellow on the outside, white on the inside. It is one thing to be a Korean-American exchange student castigated for questionable morals, and quite another to be a low-ranked member of a martial arts academy. Yet each morning Ho found a peculiar comfort in the succession of kicks he took to the torso and head. "There is no time to be depressed," he would later say, "when you're getting the shit kicked out of you."

The summer at the academy did more than strengthen his fighting skills. It reminded him that in the world in which he grew up the options were limited to a precious two: either you excelled, or you sank. There was no middle path. In an American context, his despondence during his freshman year made no sense; he was, after all, going not to Slippery Rock but to Yale. It may not have been his goal, but it was close. Yet close, in the Chang family, was not acceptable. Close was the taekwondo kick almost perfectly executed, the kick that brought a smack from the master with the bamboo pole. For a year Ho was lost because he had failed and could not ameliorate his sense of failure by accepting a close approximation of his dream. But that summer in Korea reminded him that he had a choice to make: to surrender; or to resume the purposeful struggle of his life.

Back at Yale Ho broke with his girlfriend. He did not want distractions. In the lost months of his freshman year, when his days proceeded aimlessly, he had felt himself no more than "a waste of protoplasm." But now he threw himself into his studies. He trained six hours a day. Yet he also began learning, painfully, that effort does not always mean triumph. He got only a C in organic chemistry. He rose as far as the quarter-finals at the Olympic trials before being defeated. Yet there was satisfaction even in his disappointments, because they had come through sacrifice and diligence.

He spent time between classes working with autistic children and volunteering at a hospital emergency room. During the summer he worked at a health clinic in New York's Chinatown and the following year answered phones for an AIDS hot line. Ho saw the work, especially in Chinatown, not only as a way to enhance his medical school applications, but as a way of deepening a connection with other Asians. The summer in Korea had served an additional purpose, which was to remind him where he fit in America. What he could not find during the academic year at New Haven he sought in lower Manhattan during the summer.

Ho also applied to assist professors in research projects. Research is not unlike cathedral building. Nothing happens quickly and there is no assurance that great results will come in your time. Still, Ho applied to join an experiment on the effect of lithium on rat brains, and was rewarded with the seemingly dubious task of killing the rats, extracting and analyzing their RNA, and putting in sixteen-hour shifts monitoring incubators and counting machinery. That he was willing to devote the hours on this, a necessary step on the path to becoming a doctor, made his next choice all the more curious. It was especially so for his parents, who were not pleased when he came home and announced that though he was graduating *magna cum laude*, he had spotted a poster for Teach for America in the Yale library and had committed himself to two years in an inner-city classroom.

It would have been pointless telling his parents his true motive, which was the desire to spend two years of his life doing what he wanted to do. Medical school, he reasoned, would be a grind, eclipsed only by his internship and residency. "I needed to do something for me," he says. "Entering medical school would be the end of my personal life."

He was not proposing a year of travel or teaching wind surfing at Club Med. Ho was going to teach, because that is what he desired. He told his parents that the experience would look good on his medical school applications. "I couldn't argue that this would be good for me," he says.

Unable to stop him, Ho's parents pressed him to take a job offered him by a New Jersey prep school. But this time he would not do what they wanted him to do. These two years were his.

*   *   *

After school, Mr. Chang teaches taekwondo. The gymnasium at Satellite East is given over to the Jackie Robinson Center, where children come not to run aimlessly, but to learn athletic skills. The boys swing their arms and kick their legs beneath posters of Magic Johnson and Michael Jordan. The girls learn to skip rope double dutch. Mr. Chang appears, barefoot, in his white taekwondo uniform.

"Have a seat," he barks.

The boys slowly sink to the floor.

"I don't hear you," snaps Mr. Chang.

The boys answer, "Yes sir!"

"Stand up."

The boys rush to their feet.

"Sit down!"

First, says Mr. Chang, it is time for meditation. Meditation does not mean talking or giggling or peering out of the corner of your eye at your friend. It means closing your eyes and concentrating. The boys squeeze their eyes shut and some rest their hands on their knees and press their fingertips together, the way people meditate on TV.

"We will respect our elders," Mr. Chang begins. The boys repeat the words.

"I cannot hear you!"

"We will respect our elders!"

"We will strive to endeavor!" chants Mr. Chang.

"We will never surrender!"

In unison, the boys repeat what Mr. Chang says. He orders them to open their eyes. He bows toward them, smartly, from the waist. The boys awkwardly bob their heads and torsos and steal glances at the girls skipping rope.

"*Chumbae,*" Mr. Chang barks in Korean. The boys pull themselves to attention, feet at shoulder width, arms crossed at the waist and hands balled into fists.

"*Cheryut.*" Mr. Chang is prepared for combat. He snaps his left arm ramrod straight. His left leg is back, his right leg bent at the knee. The boys watch Mr. Chang execute a savage kick to an imaginary head. Together, they go, "ooooo," as Mr. Chang sweeps his right leg forward and kicks it high. Then they try. Some fall down. Mr. Chang looks at the boys on the floor and says, "Ten push-ups." The boys who kicked before Mr. Chang ordered the kick also do ten push-ups.

Mr. Chang walks through the ranks, examining each boy's fighting stance. He adjusts their arms and legs until they are right. Some of the boys cannot figure out how to bend one leg and keep the other straight. Mr. Chang tells them, "If you do not bend it I will break it for you."

He splits the class in half for a relay race. The losers do twenty push-ups. He tells the boys, "Nothing comes easily."

But the boys cannot seem to get the hang of what Mr. Chang is telling them, that is except for one named Alfonso, whose movements are crisp and strong. While the other boys struggle to kick and punch and return to their fighting positions, Alfonso moves with the assurance of one so practiced in the art that the steps and blows seem to emanate from within. Alfonso began to study taekwondo before he came to Mr. Chang's class and Mr. Chang can see how well he has absorbed the principles of discipline and strength that taekwondo seeks to instill. "He has respect for the martial art, for the teacher and for himself," Mr. Chang later says, "and for the role taekwondo plays in his life." Though he is not in his earth science class, Mr. Chang was not surprised to hear that Alfonso is a fine student. He asks Alfonso to come to the center of the room and demonstrate a basic set of kicks and blows.

The other boys shift in their places, watching Alfonso. They lean forward and back and move from side to side. They cannot sustain a position, as Mr. Chang and Alfonso can. Alfonso moves past them, his eyes looking straight ahead, his body coiled. Mr. Chang offers suggestions in a quiet voice.

The class ends with Mr. Chang's reminder that taekwondo is meant only for self-defense. Then he begins, "I will respect my elders," and the boys sing-song along.

Later, on the subway heading to Manhattan, Mr. Chang says, "I worry about them and their futures."

*   *   *

In his first year of teaching Ho Chang believed he could help all his students. He prepared his lessons furiously, only to come to class and learn that half that day's homework assignments were not done. He called parents only to be told that yes, they were aware that their child had not done their homework or had failed yet another test and they would speak to them about it. He scheduled review sessions. When only ten out of his 100 students showed up to prepare for a test that most would fail he told them, "You should feel ashamed." As he spoke he could sense that all he was doing was sounding like another teacher reminding his students that they were failures.

Still, there were moments when he could see interest budding, when he'd tell them about the importance of learning science and the students would get excited at the prospect of running experiments. One student named Jason could not sit still but was nonetheless fascinated with physics. He asked who the famous physicists were and when Ho listed their names he said, "I want to be better than Einstein." Jason wanted to know what schools good physicists went to and Ho told him about Harvard, MIT and Cal Tech. Then, seizing his opportunity, he asked Jason how he planned to get into these schools and Jason said that he would have to study. And with that the moment ended.

Only one student said "Fuck you" to Ho's face, but that was early on, before he had learned about not letting students bait him. His students were for the most part passive. Ho could not seem to make them understand that their passivity might deny them what they wanted. What they wanted, he believed, were things that they could have immediately, which was why Nintendo, with its instant feedback, was so alluring, especially when compared with the distant rewards of schoolwork.

One day Ho asked the class what they desired. A nice house, said one. A Mercedes, said another. And how, Ho asked, do you legitimately intend to pay for these things. The students replied that they'd get a job, at which point Ho reminded them that nice houses and Mercedes-Benz were not cheap. They would need jobs that paid a lot of money. The students nodded and said they understood him, but Ho saw that they were just telling him what they sensed he wanted to hear.

"Last year I tried to make a difference in every student," he says. "Now in my own mind I gauge, How much work do I need to do for this kid?" He makes this assessment based upon how much work he senses the student is willing to do.

Yet even a glimmer of interest was enough. Last year he had a student foisted upon him who'd been bounced out of another school because he had broken into a teacher's car, torn up the upholstery and poured motor oil over the inside. The teacher had said something to the boy that bothered him.

But Ho believed that the student was not the dunce and menace everyone else saw. He could see how bright he was, and so he pushed him. On one test he scored among the top in the class and afterward Ho told him, "See, this is what can happen. You are not stupid." On the next test the boy got a forty-five and Ho understood what had happened. The boy had studied, and succeeded and then recognized that he was going to pay a price for his diligence. His friends were going to start telling him that he was "acting white." There was seemingly little to gain and much to lose by being studious. Studious people were nerds and no one wanted to be called a nerd, not even someone with a reputation for violent behavior who came to school with a four-inch gash on his arm that he got when he broke into a teacher's car.

The nerds were outsiders, like Lilanne, who was Ho's favorite student last year. Lilanne had transferred from Catholic school because her parents could no longer afford the tuition. She did not fit in at Satellite East, even among students were considered nerds by all the other students in the district. Lilanne liked to learn and worked hard and often sat alone in the cafeteria. One day she came to him crying, because another teacher was giving her a hard time. Ho listened to her story and told her, "I am honored that you came and discussed it with me." After that Lilanne had lunch in his room every day.

But there were no students like Lilanne this term. Instead there was Barry, who had a million questions that he wanted Ho to answer. But then at least Barry wanted to learn.

*   *   *

Janine Bempechat has studied students like Ho and students like Barry, trying to better understand what drives one, and leaves the other seeing no reason to do no more than the least. I tell her Ho's story, about his demanding parents, his despondence during his first year at Yale, his renewal and also about the way he tries to motivate his students in the same rigorous, uncompromising way he drove himself. "What's he's discovering," she says, "is that it's not working."

Bempechat, a professor at the Harvard Graduate School of Education, studies motivation — why students of roughly equal intelligence will perform so differently. Motivation inevitably raises the question of comparison, not only within the classroom, but between societies. It is no secret that students in Japan and Korea, for instance, consistently eclipse American students on certain standardized tests. Whether or not one accepts those criteria as valid, there is little question that East Asian students spend far more of their lives working at school than do their American counterparts.

Japanese and Korean students are held up as the icons of scholastic rigor and discipline, and indeed, little matters as much in those students' lives as the grades they get in school. The reason is simple. Those grades determine their futures: By the time they are poised to graduate from high school, the courses of their lives are all but decided by the scores they achieved. In the almost five years I spent in Japan and Korea, I was always a little unnerved by the thought of what my prospects in life might have been — a B student in high school and college, not enough certainly to gain admission to one of the better universities, and therefore in all likelihood consigned to a future in a small to medium-sized trading company. There are no second chances in Japan and Korea. Success in school not only means a well-paying job, but a position of respect. That it has been this way for many hundreds of years makes it hard to imagine America one day revering education quite the same way, hard to imagine institutionalizing respect for education in a society that offers so many other means of gaining respect.

High school is not always a happy time in Japan and Korea. Indeed, each spring, there are stories in both countries of students who kill themselves. In the zero-sum game of scholastic achievement in East Asia, suicide is the final recourse of the teenager caught between his aspirations and his failure. The suicides bring laments, but no fundamental change in the system.

There are parallels in America, ones with which Bempechat is only too familiar. She grew up in New York, in a Jewish family that considered pretty good unacceptable. Her parents made it clear to her that she had no choice but to excel at school. There was no family money for her to rely upon, no family business for her to run, no smooth route to a comfortable life. The only way to that life was school, which meant that she was expected to perform. That attitude does not always make adolescence fun, she says. But then fun was not the issue. Now, a generation later, she finds herself often taking an equally tough line. She tells the story of a friend who came to her, worried about her son. The son played on his school hockey team. He loved hockey, loved the feeling of being part of a team and, at an age when it matters so much, knowing who his friends were. But his grades began slipping and the friend asked Bempechat what she should do.

"Pull him out of hockey," she replied, to which her friend responded that that would be disastrous: his self-esteem would suffer a catastrophic blow. Besides, she added, no other parent she asked advised so draconian a solution.

Perhaps Bempechat was being harsh. Perhaps the end of hockey would have made the young man so angry and resentful, that his grades might have slid even lower. But in hearing Bempechat tell the story I was struck by the clarity of her thinking: school was what mattered. Of course it was important to make friends and feel good and build a rounded life. But not, she maintained, at the expense of schoolwork. The message to this student would have been unequivocal: in this case, hockey is a reward earned in the classroom. It is not a right.

That is just what Ho Chang's parents would have done, had his grades begun slipping. And though Ho might have stomped around the house and sat on his bed, cursing them, he would have known that the only way he could have what he wanted was by doing his best in class. But that worked for Ho, and others like him, who, Bempechat says, regardless of race, class, or income, believe they have no other choice. What they share, she says, is persistence, a willingness to push themselves and not give up when things get hard and failure feels imminent. They are also willing to delay gratification, to see not only the present but the future and the connection between their effort and their faraway dreams.

Asian students, she says, are not smarter. But they and their parents believe that if they work harder they can become smarter. The view is just the opposite among American students, who see long hours of schoolwork as a sign that they are not very bright at all, because smart kids should know the answers without straining.

These are students who, in Bempechat's view, are reared by parents who may truly believe in the value of education, but who also want to see smiles on their children's faces. She cites a study in which a group of American parents were asked what grade would satisfy them in a test whose average score was seventy-five. Most said they'd be satisfied with a grade eight to ten points lower. Asian parents replied that they'd be satisfied with grades eight to ten points higher.

To accomplish that the Asian parents could be expected to be like Ho's parents — defining his life and then looming over his shoulder. But then Asian parents do not bring their children up to be independent of them. Quite the contrary. Children grow up believing that there exists an unwritten contract between themselves and their parents: the parents will give them everything; they will place them at the center of their lives. And in return the child, in eternal gratitude, will keep his parents in the center of his heart and his thoughts. The idea of raising children to one day leave home — physically and emotionally — applies in America, not Asia, just as in America, countless children are brought up to be popular and smart and good athletes and capable of perhaps also holding down an after-school job. "I don't think education matters to us nearly as much as we say it does," Bempechat says.

Besides if American children do not do as well as they might in school, there are always second chances. There are — or were — always new career paths, or training programs. There are always new places to move to, new cities and states where all that will be asked of them will be the year of their graduation and the name of the school. No one will ask their grades, or whether their grades were earned in advanced placement or remedial classes.

That these questions go unasked, that a rigorous course load often goes unmentioned and unrewarded, is especially disturbing to such education advocates as Chester E. Finn, Jr., the former director of the Education Excellence Network, author of *We Must Take Charge: Our Schools and Our Future*, and now a member of Christopher Whittle's proposed private school system, The Edison Project. Finn does not blame students for seeking the easy way. After all, he says, why should they push themselves if they'll have nothing to show for it.

"I think these kids by and large are behaving rationally," he says. "Except for kids trying to go to the Yales, Princetons or Stanfords, most young Americans don't reap any tangible benefits for pushing themselves for good grades. It's all the same whether they took the honors classes or skated by. Should the typical sixteen-year-old rework his history paper or go out with his friends? If the minimum is good enough for your purposes the minimum is what you'll do."

Finn castigates schools and school systems for seeking the balm of good news, and spreading it like gospel. "We give kids false good news about how well they're doing. We tell them they're doing great and we tell their parents much the same thing."

But what would happen, he suggests, if colleges — not just the elite schools, but the many other good colleges — made entrance requirements far more rigorous? What would happen if students knew that they were going to have to have something more than a diploma and passing grades to gain admission to college? What would happen if those students knew that a tough course was weighed more heavily than a easy one? Then, Finn argues, students would see that there was a connection between their performance in school and getting something they wanted. He takes the argument a step further, applying it to the workplace. If a student knew that a prospective employer would one day ask what kind of grades he or she got and, what kinds of courses he or she took, that student would have a clear reason to do more than merely graduate.

Here Finn parts with those he calls the educational "progressives," those who argue that ultimately, the best motivated student is the one driven not by external demands, but because of an intrinsic desire to learn and excel. The progressives, too, fault not the student, but school. They argue that if all school asks is the ability to recall a set of facts soon after they are digested, students will see no need to do more. And why should they? Students learn at an early age how the game is played. They learn to do what is asked of them. To expect them to want to do more without reward, and without allowing them to truly experience the joy of learning, is foolish and unfair.

Yet by and large schools cling to the traditional methods of instruction and evaluation, which means that such intrinsic motivation works only with rare student who works well in school as it is now devised. Without that sort of mind, or that kind of significant reform, Finn argues that students need a carrot. "I believe that is far too weak a reed to rely upon for most kids to learn chemistry, history, geometry and literature and right down the list," he says of an internal desire to learn. "We have to appeal to their self-interest — more money, entrance into something you crave."

Yet despite the pressure he'd like to see applied, Finn still finds himself in a quandary: he cannot quite bring himself to apply the stick, to follow the Asian model of both reward and punishment for failure to achieve. "I'm torn because I believe in second chances," he says. "I'd give them a second and third chance to do well in school. Sure you can come back to school again. But eventually you have to demonstrate that you've learned it."

America, in a sense, wants it both ways: it wants its children to do well in school, but not at too great a cost to their maturity and happiness. If Japan and Korea are, in a profound sense, unforgiving of mediocrity — if you do not get into college you drive a bus; you had your choice; you blew it — then, perhaps, he argues, America has grown too forgiving. Finn does not want to stop being forgiving. He just wants students to know that if they do well, not adequately, but well, they will get something very desirable and real for their trouble.

*   *   *

Barry is in the principal's office, being fitted for a belt. Today he came to school with his pants falling down. The boys at Satellite East must wear black slacks, a white shirt and tie; the girls wear black skirts and white blouses. Some wear black cardigans with the Satellite East logo over their hearts. The Muslim girls cover their hair.

A secretary finds a belt from the Salvation Army and slips it around Barry's slim waist. Barry stands in the middle of the room, surrounded by middle-aged women. He smiles an embarrassed smile. Katherine Corbett, the principal, glances across the room at Barry and then continues talking about excellence and motivation. Though Barry confounds Ho Chang, he is a type with whom she is acquainted. "I rule this house," she says. "I'm the mother. They call me Mom Corbett. I'm not going to let you settle for less."

She is a formidable woman, tall and broad and capable of instantly quieting a noisy hallway by the simple act of striding out of her office. When Corbett came to Satellite East, the school emphasized the arts. The arts still matter at Satellite East, but after the schoolwork is done.

Corbett talks of "attainable goals" drawn from conversations with teachers about what they think is possible, and then seeing how those goals correspond with the requirements laid down by the state of New York. But she does not want a school where teachers teach for the tests. When students founder she talks with them, asking them what they want — not about college, which feels like light years away — but something more immediate, like what high school they might want to attend. Selection at the city's better schools is competitive and Corbett knows the prospect of Stuyvesant or Music and Art as opposed to the fearsome place that is Thomas Jefferson can provide a powerful impetus.

But even if she can plant in her students' minds the dream of such a school, she cannot always be sure that the dream will survive. It is not just the street, or even the considerable pressure of peers that she most fears. It is parents.

The parents who have pushed their children to qualify for Satellite East are not indifferent. But often they are overwhelmed. Corbett asks them to review and sign their children's homework, not merely ask if the homework is done before the television goes on. The parents tell her that they too are in school and that their schooling comes after work and besides there are younger children at home who are equally demanding of their time. The parents are dreamers, too, and they are stretched. One casualty of the pace of their lives are the needs of their teenagers. They tell Corbett "they're old enough" to take care of themselves, believing as American parents often believe, that responding to an adolescent's neediness might keep that child forever bound to home.

Besides, it is one thing to help a child trying to understand basic arithmetic and quite another to answer questions about geometry and the periodic table of elements. "They're not confident when their child asks questions about earth science," Corbett says. "They say, 'Ask the teacher.'" What makes this all the more sad is that these are parents who want so much for their children.

"They tell them, 'You can be whatever you want to be,'" Corbett says. "But they have to put legs on that vision. How do you get them to take their children to the museum?"

Often, you don't. So the school does it for them. Corbett has arranged trips not only to the Ellis Island museum and to the Museum of Modern Art — where the children not only look at paintings, but meet the curators — but to such events as the swearing-in ceremony at the New York Bar Association. Corbett regards such ceremonies as a crucial ingredient in her students' education — one that shows them how the future might look. She does not stop there. In the hallway she's assembled the school's Wall of Fame, photographs of graduates who have gone on to college. She schedules visits to such schools as Howard University, which was how Ho Chang got the idea of a trip to Yale.

Ho wanted his eighth graders to dream big dreams. He wanted them to think not just of New York Tech or the state university at Geneseo, admirable as those aspirations might be. He wanted them to see the future as he had seen it, or rather as his parents saw it for him. So he took his proposal to Corbett who told him to make the necessary arrangements.

He persuaded a roommate who'd been active in the Black Students Alliance to arrange for twenty-five hosts, undergraduates who would let the Satellite East students crash in their rooms. He arranged for meetings with other black students, for a dance at a black fraternity, for tickets to the Yale-Penn football game and, of course, for classes that his students might attend.

The trip was by invitation only, the invitations extended, after a meeting of the faculty, to those with the best grades and behavior evaluations. As the trip approached, Ho was peppered with requests from those who hadn't been invited but who nonetheless wanted to know what they'd have to do come along. One offered a five dollar bribe.

The forty-three who were chosen set off by bus on a Thursday, right after school. Dressed in their school uniforms — this did not go over well; people wanted to get dressed up — they headed north, out of Brooklyn and then Manhattan and finally, on Interstate 95, heading to New Haven. When Ho announced that they were leaving New York and entering a new state they asked "What state?"

Some looked out the window, at the distant church steeples and expanse of uninterrupted green. Most leaned over one another's seats, playing pocket computer games. They stopped at a roadside McDonald's for dinner — "Can we order anything we want?" — and after an enforced nap arrived on campus in time to see people in costume, ready for Halloween.

That night, after he'd finally tracked down all the hosts and checked which lectures might be open, Ho made his rounds. Some hosts had taken their guests out for pizza but by eleven o'clock most everyone was in, though not necessarily asleep. Many, already in pajamas, stayed up well into the night, asking questions about life at college.

The next morning Ho split the group in two and sent them off to class. He led one group first to an introductory psychology course, where the professor was lecturing about IQ and intelligence. The professor lectured in a modified Socratic form — asking questions that the class knew to be rhetorical. But Ho's students did not know this. They knew that in Mr. Chang's class the student who did not have his hand up was the student Mr. Chang called on. And so it was that as the professor posed a question about measuring the impact of heredity on intelligence, a question she fully expected to answer herself, several hands of eighth-graders shot up. Unruffled, she called on Jameel.

"You gotta like talk to the parents and ask questions," he said. "See if they're smart and all."

"You're on the right track," replied the professor, much to Ho's pleasure and Jameel's delight. Later, Jameel would tell everyone, "I answered a question at Yale."

Ho took his students to lunch at the freshman commons, a great hall with a high ceiling, panelled walls, pillars and portraits of esteemed men long dead. Ho had been awed by the room as a freshman, by the setting, by the china and the silver. But now he was disappointed that his students did not feel as he had. Though they were free to eat as much as they wanted, few wanted seconds and fewer still, thirds. Instead, everyone wanted to know when free time began so they could go shopping for sweatshirts. Free time, Ho told them, came after the campus tour.

In the course of the day the group met with a student adviser, who told them about what Yale expected of its applicants. They saw the libraries and the classrooms and the playing fields. And then, at night, they went to a dance.

The dance was sponsored by a black fraternity and for the first hour the dance floor belonged to the students of Satellite East. No drinking was allowed, but that did not matter because the students had their music and Ho could not get over the intensity with which they danced. The undergraduates, arriving late, filtered into the room, and the eighth graders mixed easily with them at this, the first school dance many had ever attended. Dances were not held at Satellite East because of the fear of fighting.

In the weeks that followed, Ho kept asking his students what they thought of the trip. He composed a questionnaire and from it learned that virtually everyone in the group was interested in going to Yale, except for one, who wanted to go to Harvard. As the memories of Jameel's answer in class, the late night talks with their hosts and the campus tour evaporated, what remained for the group was the memory of the dance.

Soon, the bragging and talk ended and the students placed the weekend in the past. But Ho could not let go of it, until the students suggested that he give Yale a rest. So he was left to wonder about the visit's impact, whether it might indeed stir his students to dream lofty dreams, or whether it would remain a pleasant memory soon to be replaced by more immediate desires. For Ho, the weekend would become a microcosm of the year: he planted a seed and then waited, perhaps never knowing whether it might grow.

*　　　　　*　　　　　*

Mr. Chang is teaching a lesson on plotting the heating curve for water. He begins the lesson with a quiz on the periodic table of elements. It is less a test of knowledge than it is an instrument to bolster academic discipline. Mr. Chang tells the class that they should be able to answer each of the twenty questions in three seconds, which means they should be done in exactly one minute. "But," he says, "I will be gracious enough to give you three times that amount."

The test complete, Mr. Chang launches into the lesson, asking his students to copy the objective off the blackboard and then turn their eyes to the heating element and the beaker of water in the front of the room. Together they will plot the temperature at which water boils and the number of calories necessary to achieve this. He asks questions and when the answers are not right he snaps, 'incorrect,' and calls on someone else. There is no margin for error in Mr. Chang's class.

Barry sits at his desk in the front of the room, clutching a handful of felt-tip markers. He uses different colors to mark each section of his heat-plotting graph. He raises his hand with Mr. Chang's first question and does not put it down. He knows all the answers and when one of his classmates replies incorrectly he calls out, "Me. Me." The others do not make the connections between heat and calories as quickly as Barry does.

Finally, after Habib sees why boiling water does not consistently get hotter the longer it boils, after Andre overcomes his confusion about last year's experiment with boiling water and salt, Barry calls out his question.

"I went to Prospect Park. I went to look at the lake. The top of the lake was frozen. How come there was ice on the top and water on the bottom?"

Mr. Chang asks, "Can you explain it?"

Barry says, No, and Mr. Chang says, "we have no time for the explanation."

But Barry will not let go of the question. He asks it again and again but Mr. Chang does not feel he can stop to answer it.

"Can you answer my question now?" Barry asks. "Can you answer my question after this?"

Now someone else wants to know the answer to Barry's question. She says she wants to talk with him about it after class. Barry smiles and says, "After class I'm gonna be home."

The bell rings and Barry lingers but asks no more questions before going home to watch television and play Nintendo with his younger sister until their mother comes home from work. Mr. Chang switches on his antique cassette player and plays Vivaldi for the four volunteers who have remained behind to help grade the day's tests. He tells them to deduct points for misspellings and twenty-five points for everyone who forgot to write down their name.

*   *   *

If teachers, especially new teachers, teach the way they were taught, then the teacher Ho Chang emulates was the one who taught him the discipline and principles of taekwondo — his father. And what motivated Ho to do his best for this, his best teacher, was fear.

This is not to say that his father went out of his way to make his eldest son afraid, no more than Ho himself tries to frighten his students the way some teachers can. Ho does not threaten. He does not scream. Rather, he tries to do what his father did for him, which was to make him fearful of what might happen if he did not excel. For Ho, there was no doubt about what might have happened had he decided that school did not matter very much: "I sensed that my parents' love hinged on my success at school."

Whether it did is not the issue. Ho believed it to be so, and so did what he had to do to ensure that he would not jeopardize this love. It is hard to imagine a more powerful motivating tool — instilling in a very young child the idea that love is conditional. But, in the end, it is a tool with limited applications, especially with children who have not grown up quite so afraid.

The children in Ho's class, and in so many other classes in all kinds of schools and in all kinds of neighborhoods, do not know the world as he did. They do not grow up seeing it as a place without options. For Ho there was no easy way out. And though many of his students cannot envision the world that Ho grew up seeing — the Ivy League, medical school, a successful practice — they do see many other sources of pleasure that can be had with little exertion.

Ho tells them that there is more to life than they think, that they can have pleasures and rewards with lasting value, but that they must pay for these with effort that may seldom be enjoyable. He shows them the dream at New Haven and then tries to give them the tools for attaining it by making them fearful: of seeing the low grades posted next to their names, of being told they are wrong in front of everyone, of being penalized for not doing their best.

I put this philosophy to a high school student attending an alternative school for those who'd foundered in class. His name was Joe Cintron and he knew enough about failure in school to speak with authority. I told him about Ho's approach, about trying to instill a work ethic through fear. Joe believed not only that this could not work, but that it was counterproductive.

At sixteen Joe was firmly in the "progressive" camp. He did not believe in homework and testing and posting grades for their own sake. He did not believe that these fostered discipline. Rather, he argued, they just reinforced in students' minds that notion of school as a place where all that was really required was an ability to show that you can remember a set of facts or names or numbers shortly after the teacher told them to you. In the end, Joe believed, the only way you learned was when you learned on your own — when you put ideas together and found pleasure in the doing of it. The tests, he believed, could instill fear — the fear of failing. And that was a fear best avoided. So rather than taking a chance, you learned either to avoid any risk and do what was necessary not to fail, or, as too often happened, giving up and not bothering at all.

"If they feel stupid that's more reason for them to quit," Joe said. "I think he was probably brought up a certain way. His parents had their foot on his neck. That's all he knew. Maybe he thinks it's right. But it may not be."

But when I suggest to Ho Chang that perhaps his approach was not necessarily the right one, that the discipline that comes through fear works only with the already fearful, he disagrees: Who is to know what these students will take with them?

Perhaps, he says, I can plant in their minds the idea that excellence is the only goal worth pursuing. Perhaps in a year or five years or ten, they will remember having a teacher who told them they were capable of great things and these things would not come without effort. Fear, he insists, was not a bad thing. Quite the contrary, it is useful motivation.

And as with so much else in his life, Ho Chang was willing to delay his reward, the reward of seeing his effort pay off. For he had learned at home that life's great pleasures do not come quickly.

2

The Body Book

Jill Gaulding (MIT, '90)

Today Ms. Gaulding is teaching about the classification of species and that is part of the problem. It is not that her seventh graders are averse to this lesson, at least any more than they are to any lesson that does not directly touch on the subject of human reproduction. Ms. Gaulding knows this. So last night she sat up and, as so often happens, tried to find a way to make her students think that learning about the classification of species was, if not essential to their lives, nonetheless interesting.

When Jill Gaulding was in seventh grade she devoured lessons like this one. In fact she devoured anything that had to do with science. Her students do not. When she looks at her seventh graders she sees eyes staring at the ceiling, or gazing out the window or buried in an arm that lays across a desk. Ms. Gaulding's students look at her with bafflement, which too often dissolves into the slumbering eyes of the student lost, frustrated and resigned to defeat. Sometimes their looks could kill, especially if she has called their parents the night before to alert them to behavior or class work problems. They yell at her, "Why did you lie on me?" Then they tune her out, as do the sleepers, the talkers and those who rise to wander during class.

The bell rings and, lunch complete, they amble into Ms. Gaulding's room, under the big letters that spell out, "Scientists Ask Questions." They throw down their book bags, fight over chairs, tell Ms. Gaulding that they didn't start the fighting, make faces when Ms. Gaulding tells them to stop fighting, smack each other, insult each other and ask for the pass to the bathroom.

Ms. Gaulding says, "One, two, three freeze," and, knowing that the moment of silence will be short-lived, launches into classification.

"Ms. Gaulding tell him to move," whines one girl, while another with vacant eyes sucks on a baby's bottle.

"Why do we need to classify all living things?" Ms. Gaulding asks and when no one answers she asks them to turn to turn to page 82 in their ancient textbooks and look at the picture of the fish. "That is an ugly fish," she says, drawing out the "u," hoping it will make them laugh. Ms. Gaulding has learned that if she is not entertaining her students they will switch her off like a dull sit-com. "The fisherman noticed that not only was it ugly but unusual. Scientists thought this fish was extinct."

"It was dead?" someone asks.

"No it wasn't," she says, gently. "And that was the big discovery. Without a classification system it would be just another ugly fish."

She has them. She asks, "Okay, question number two: Why do we need scientific names?"

This, she knows, is risky. If she asks a question that involves their having to think they might well get upset that the answer does not come quickly and give up and turn their eyes away from her. She tries. "Everybody think. What would be the advantage?"

"I don't see any," says one.

"Okay, that's a fine answer. What's the disadvantage?"

She senses she can wait no longer. She pushes on. "Okay, I've discovered an animal I call the cat. I'm talking to a scientist in Spain and he tells me he's discovered an animal he calls *el gato*. But if we both use the scientific name *felis domestica* . . ."

"That's a ten dollar word," someone calls out.

"That's definitely a ten dollar word," she says. "It's a twenty dollar word because it's got two parts. If I came to Hayward and asked how his felis domestica was he might smack me."

Maybe the twenty dollar names are useful only for scientists, she says. Maybe there are of no use to the rest of us. But they are a way of talking with each other, a way of making ourselves understood anyplace in the world. The words may be elusive; but we all try to make order of our worlds.

Ms. Gaulding says, Imagine all the things in your closet. You want to make sense of them. You want to take stock of what you have. How do you begin? To help them, she has written across the board a scheme for organizing their possessions: there are the broad categories of shoes and clothes; beneath shoes are two sub-categories — sneakers and dress shoes and beneath those, different categories for the colors of the shoes.

"Alison, how many levels can you point out?" Ms. Gaulding asks.

Alison wearily replies, "Can I go to the bathroom?"

Ms. Gaulding plows on. A boy sitting near the window raises and lowers the shade. Another takes the heart and brain from the plastic full-sized human torso and shows it to his friend. Alison, returned from the bathroom, walks across the room to chat.

And then it happens. Ms. Gaulding asks a question that intrigues them: "How would you divide all the living things in the world? Where would the split be?"

A hand shoots up, followed by five others.

"Things with legs and things that don't have legs," someone says.

"Good," says Ms. Gaulding.

"Plants and animals."

"Things too small to see."

"An atom."

"An egg."

"A lady bug."

Now they're calling out.

"A cell."

"A cell is the smallest living thing."

"A flea."

"No," howls a classmate.

Ms. Gaulding reminds them that for something to be an animal it has to be multi-cellular and must eat food. Then she says, "the last one is something you find in the kitchen if you left bread out too long."

Most everyone raises a hand. Ms. Gaulding calls on Wallace. Wallace sits in the back of the room when he comes to class, which is once every ten days. Wallace is a chubby teenager who likes to talk to the people sitting next to him. But now he had a hand up, and Ms. Gaulding spots him.

"Bacteria?" he says, searching.

The chorus grows louder with Wallace's wrong answer. Everyone wants Ms. Gaulding to call their name. They call out, "Me. Me. I know."

But Wallace is staying with it and Ms. Gaulding is staying with Wallace. He is squeezing his eyes together, seeking the answer.

"Oh yeah, yeah, fungi," he calls out.

And then it is over. Wallace slips a pen behind his ear and lowers his head into his arms to doze.

Today, in these forty-five minutes, each student in Ms. Gaulding's Life Science class will raise his or her hand at least once and call out to Ms. Gaulding the words, "I know." They will plead with her to notice them, to recognize them for understanding.

The moments are fleeting, but they are what keep Ms. Gaulding going, between the walkers and the shouters and the parade to the bathroom. Ms. Gaulding's day began with taking her turn filling in for a Spanish teacher who'd left after the first week of school because a student had knocked out his teeth. It is January and a permanent replacement has not yet been found. Ms. Gaulding's job was to stand in the classroom and weather the ignominy of a student hitting her when she asked her to stand away from the window and stop yelling down to a friend.

Yet it is not necessarily a bad day. It is, at times, a very good day. It is like most days for Ms. Gaulding at Francis Scott Key Junior High School in Brooklyn's Bedford-Stuyvesant, the largest ghetto neighborhood in New York. Today will begin with possibilities and end with rigorous self-criticism and examination. And in between will be moments like the one with Wallace, moments when Ms. Gaulding sees more than words in the Nina Willis Walter poem she has taped to the wardrobe door.

Our minds
Are little pools,
Shallow little rain pools,
And yet, sometimes they do reflect
The stars.

*   *   *

Jill Gaulding did not make things easy for herself. She had left a Ph.D. program in linguistics at her alma mater, M.I.T, having wearied of academia. Unsure of what she wanted to do with her life, she applied for a place in Teach for America, hoping that she might find her path in this, a classroom of a different sort.

As an undergraduate and then as a graduate student, Jill studied the acquisition of language, or more specifically, how language comes to represent meaning in our minds. She was a scientist not only by training, but by inclination. In eighth grade, when other students turned away from slides under their microscopes, Jill marveled at the construction of cells, at the idea that she was seeing how the world was put together. "It was," she says, "like finding out about God." Having studied the components upon which the world is built and then how we make sense of that world through language, she now found herself caught up by the equally compelling question of how children learn.

Her instructors at Teach for America's summer institute championed the idea of "active learning," the idea that true understanding happens only when the student, regardless of age, comes to know a body of knowledge intimately enough to make it his or her own. Learning, the theory holds, does not occur when a student masters the trick of recalling a series of concepts as delineated by the teacher — and then performs the much-applauded trick of repeating them on a test. Rather, it means that that student absorbs an idea independently, which occurs when students find answers not for a teacher's questions, but for their own. The example of such learning that Jill especially liked was a scientific one: the sweater and heat. Students, she learned, often came to school convinced that sweaters kept them warm because there was something inherent in the garment that generated heat.

That theory was like so many of the other erroneous but nonetheless significant conclusions that children draw in their pre-school years — significant because they provide the basis for learning. What matters when a child comes to school is not so much the ability to write his or her name or to know the letters of the alphabet, as recited on Sesame Street. That represents little more than parroting information that Mom and Dad deem important. Rather it is coming to school eager to learn, or more specifically to continue learning, to continue their ongoing work of discovery.

Children are forever making sense of their world around them. They devise theories and test them, theories on interpersonal relations ("If I cry, mommy will come running") and physics ("If I touch the radiator my hand will hurt"). The theories may be flawed in that they do not necessarily explain the world the way it actually works. But children believe them, that is until they come to school, where they are told that all the marvelous theories they'd developed over the past four or five years are wrong and that the tall stranger holding the chalk in the front of the room is there to set them straight.

The problem, Jill came to see, was two-fold. First, the children-cum-students are made to feel like dunces for seeing things wrong. And then they are asked to forget what they believed and accept a different — and often contradictory — theory as fact, simply because a person who looked like a parent told them to do so. The teacher tells them: This is the truth because smart adults say so; let's do an experiment to show that we are right. Learning then proceeds not from a question — and therefore out of curiosity — but from the assumption of certainty that students are expected to accept. But children can be stubborn: Though this person in charge speaks with assurance about the validity of his or her theory, the words are not always taken as gospel, as Jill discovered in the matter of the heat-generating sweater.

She learned that when children come to school believing that a sweater gives off heat they cling to that theory, despite a welter of evidence to the contrary. A teacher can conduct any number of experiments, proving his or her "truth" — that heat is generated by the body and not the garment. And still, the student will insist that there is something in that sweater that keeps them from shivering on a chilly day. They will alter that belief not when they are sufficiently beaten down to surrender — then they'll just humor the teacher and satisfy the district requirements by telling those in charge what they want to hear — but when they've tested this new theory to their own satisfaction. The knowledge, the truth, thereby becomes not the teacher's truth, but theirs. From such a premise the great discoveries of science have been born, a fact that is lost on the educational establishment that in practice holds that should students come to class with a set of erroneous theories the teacher is mandated to debunk and replace them with a wholly different set before the final exams.

The evolution of a new theory on sweaters may take weeks. It may take more than simply placing a thermometer under a sweater and then under a student armpit. In fact, Jill discovered, it may take weeks of experiment, of trial and error and resistance. And should the teacher, weary of the repetition, baffled by the illogic of the student world view and anxious about keeping pace with the state-mandated curriculum, stray and say, "look, we've done this twelve times, you're wrong, I'm right, the book says so," that student will be about as convinced of the validity of that argument as the Royal Academy of Science was when Darwin told them what he learned on the Galapagos Islands. The Academy's members had to learn it for themselves, and until they did they weren't going to believe him.

The difference, of course, is that the Royal Academy was in a position of authority and students are not. The institution of school places them firmly in the subordinate position, which may do wonders for order but little for understanding. They will leave school still convinced that there is something in their sweaters that keeps them warm.

So it was, then, that Jill headed east to Brooklyn, her head filled with visions of eager eighth graders at Francis Scott Key Junior High School devising and testing their theories in such a way that they might truly learn. But what she hadn't counted on — and what no one in that summer institute had warned her — was that her students had been conditioned by six years of school to see her as yet another in a long line of grown-ups forcing down their throats a version of the truth that had long since stopped mattering.

*   *   *

By the spring she was ready to quit. "Do I want to quit. Yes," she said one afternoon as mice scampered around her room after yet another difficult class. "Did I make a commit-ment? Yes. Do I feel guilty? Yes."

The term had begun smoothly. On the first day of class-es she joined the teachers, parents and nervous students who listened as their names were called out and mispronounced for home room assignments. The New York City Board of Education does assist teachers with their first day of class by distributing guidelines for getting started — reciting the classroom rules and regulations, having the students write down their schedules, giving them assigned seats, filling out emergency contact cards. Classes, too, went well. Students appeared eager. They listened when she spoke. But Jill was not content merely speaking. She wanted them to learn.

Soon the troubles began. Or rather, the manifestations of the troubles that had existed beneath that early veneer of calm, began to surface. Experiment days, the days Jill had envisioned as true, "hands on" science, became exercises in futility with Jill struggling to explain the most basic instruc-tions to students who showed no interest in what she had to say, and sometimes no comprehension. Instead they battled each other for possession of the meager supplies.

Moving from rows of desks to clusters designed for cooperative work proved as intractable as seating at a Middle East peace conference. The hall pass became like a baton in a relay-race, passed from hand to hand. Students rose to walk across the room and talk with friends. When Jill told them to stop talking they insisted that they hadn't said a word. They wrote "bitch" on the blackboard. When she told them to sit they told her, "fuck off." No longer was the issue one of active learning. It was quickly becoming a matter of survival. Jill's instructors at the summer institute had said that all any teacher needed to maintain discipline was a good lesson. Classroom management, they insisted, could not be taught; it could only be learned through experience. Jill prepared her lessons. She stayed up late at night making scores of indi-vidual experiments. And then, in class, her students took the experiments she made for them and squashed them under their shoes.

Desperate, she offered rewards. She brought in movies about science. But when she showed them *Fantastic Voyage* — a science-fiction journey through a human body — they told her "we don't want your dumb movies," because they wanted *Robocop 2* instead. She made them brownies. They told her the brownies "stink." When a student told her what a bad teacher she was, Jill said to herself, "God, you're right. I'm terrible."

It was not just a matter of supplies, or support, although she had neither. Beyond the half-dozen beakers, worn posters and almost-working microscopes at her disposal, was a catalog called Teacher's Choice, from which she could order up to $250 of what appeared to be dated and over-priced supplies that might or might not arrive during the term. Like many teachers she spent her own money on sup-plies — $100 on Ziploc bags and food coloring for experi-ments. As for support, the mentor she was promised by Teach for America never materialized — a problem that was not hers alone and that Teach for America acknowledged. Jill's colleagues offered what encouragement they could, which often came down to suggestions on how to make a class so afraid they'd stay in their seats.

But the children did not fear her. And Jill was lost, clos-eted away in an overheated, mouse-infested classroom, in a school that was under review by the state department of edu-cation because of its declining test scores. She was given, in addition to her first-day guidelines, a manual titled "Essential Learning Outcomes," the board of education's standards for what children had to know. How she taught them was her business. It became the board's business only at test time, when the students were expected to show how well they'd absorbed the required facts.

The manual offered not only a listing of mandated con-cepts, but also a timetable for instruction. Unsure of herself and not given to battling the system, Jill began the term with a keen eye on the requirements and another on her ever-more elusive students, who could have cared less about "Essential Learning Outcomes."

She quickly learned that the preferred method of instruction at Francis Scott Key Junior High School was the lesson copied off the board. The students would file into the room, take their seats, take out their notebooks, and copy down what the teacher had written. Homework was based on what they'd copied. Later they would be tested. The method was popular because it meant that the teacher did not have to focus on instruction, and could concentrate instead on discipline. Second to copying-as-instruction, was the lecture — also popular because the teacher could keep the students in rows and could ensure that they did not say a word unless they were called upon.

Having come eager to try something different, Jill found herself both assigning copying and lecturing, if only to keep the class from spinning hopelessly out of control. She hated doing it. Copying was punitive, and lecturing not only dull but useless. All it accomplished was reinforcing in her students' minds the idea that knowledge was not something gained actively, but absorbed as it floated from the single fount of information — the teacher — to their occasionally alert ears. Neither method asked anything of them, other than to hold a set of facts in their heads long enough to spill them out at test time.

What especially troubled Jill was the passivity with which her manageable students regarded school. School was like television, in that all you had to do was sit and watch. You didn't have to exert yourself. And the longer they spent doing nothing, the more they feared the prospect of being forced to take an active role in learning. Thinking, asking questions, answering questions all meant risk and risk meant possible failure. What was there to be gained in feeling like more of a failure than most of them already did? And so they sat and stared at the ceiling or talked with their friends and did the very minimum expected of them, which was showing up.

The result was a class in disarray, filled with students who saw no reason whatsoever for bothering to try. In truth, not every student was intent on mayhem. The trouble invariably began with a core group of students who could not sit next to a classmate without smacking, taunting or making faces. From there the problem would spread like a brush-fire on a parched field, engulfing student after student until Jill found herself breaking up fights — and sometimes accidentally getting punched in the stomach for her trouble — marking students for detention or sending them to the principal's office. Soon she stopped sending them to the office because the office people sent them back. "For me it was like, they're doing something I don't want them to do and I've given them a penalty and they're still doing it and there are no more penalties."

Into this walked Jill Gaulding, whose idea of behaving badly in eighth grade was once to subtly tease a teacher into thinking she was dressing poorly by complimenting her on her outfit day after day, and then stopping. Jill, who grew up on Bainbridge Island near Seattle and who sailed through school with nothing but A's, disliked this teacher because she was not particularly good at her job. And that was how she now saw herself.

"It's depressing and degrading that what you thought you were good at you're not," she said. "I've never failed before. Ninety-nine percent of the time is spent thinking of devious ways to control them. But how can you blame them? Deep down inside they want to learn. They're frightened."

But not of her. They did not listen; they did not behave; they did not seem to care. Nothing she tried, not in instruction or discipline, worked, including the method she had carried with her into the classroom, and then, overwhelmed by the growing chaos, abandoned. But now, in desperation, she would try again. She recognized she had nothing to lose; she and her students were foundering, and no one in the administration seemed to care what she did so long as there was minimal noise coming from her room.

So Jill came to class one day with a balloon and a knitting needle. The class, momentarily attentive, watched as she held up the balloon and inserted the needle where the rubber was thickest. They braced for the explosion that did not come.

"See what can happen when you look at things in a different way?" she asked. Then she told them about the book they were going to write together, the one they'd call, The Body Book.

*   *   *

All Eleanor Duckworth asks of her students is that they watch the moon. There are no rules. There are no tests, or pop quizzes or term papers on the nature of the moon. There is only watching and learning.

Duckworth asks her students to look at the moon in different ways, and then to note its patterns. She does not grade their note taking. Rather, she asks only that they record what they see. They can do this in a manner of their own choosing. Some draw pictures of the moon at different points in the sky. One student transcribed poems about the moon. Another devised names for its various shapes, calling one, "Chinese ravioli."

Duckworth's students at the Harvard Graduate School of Education often find the assignment a difficult one, in that it seems to have something to do with learning, but nothing at all with the way they've learned. She guides them, offering suggestions on how they might begin: Spend one night watching the moon's progress across the sky. Note the change in tilt. Note the place in the sky at a certain time. "I just ask them to watch it," Duckworth says. Yet her students feel lost as they look up at the darkened sky, trying to figure out how to look at the world all over again.

"In the very beginning it was too disorienting to be fun," says Lisa Schneier, now one of Duckworth's teaching assistants and one of the instructors at Teach for America's first summer institute. "I learned in school not to look at the world. That's why it felt at first strangely disorienting and later, hugely wondrous."

The wonder can be slow in coming and is often preceded by frustration and resentment at the memory of what school had always been. Duckworth is teaching her teachers-to-be how learning happens, which bears little resemblance to learning as they'd come to know it. "I'd never really looked at anything in science," Schneier says.

Duckworth's students watch the moon and begin to ask questions. The watching is not haphazard; Duckworth believes that there is a value in acquiring insights in a progression; as in any good curriculum one idea can help lead to the next. When one round of questions are answered, when they can see patterns in the habits of the moon, her students ask more questions. It is that simple. And that difficult.

But there is also something disconcerting in her method of instruction, disconcerting, that is, to those accustomed to traditional methods. How can this really be learning? And who says learning has to be fun, or at the very least moderately pleasurable? I learned, I suppose (the reasoning goes), and I didn't like it.

If an imaginary group of men once sat around a table and tried to devise a way to teach that ran contrary to every principle of the acquisition of knowledge they could not have found a truer embodiment of that desire than the way school works.

The method by which generations of American school children have been taught is "alien to the way the human species learn and to the way the human species gets excited about things," says Howard Gardner, a colleague of Duckworth's at the Harvard Graduate School of Education and the author, most recently, of *The Unschooled Mind: How Children Think and How Schools Should Teach*. It is Gardner's point, raised in such earlier books as *Frames of Mind*, that learning does not happen the same way in every mind. Different people — different children — think differently. But school insists that they all think the same, rewarding those students whose minds process information in a way roughly equivalent to the curriculum guidelines, and punishing those who cannot. The mistake too often made is that the child who is not doing what is asked of him is either lazy, indifferent, unmotivated or stupid, when in fact he or she may possess a keen mind that simply processes information not in the linear fashion celebrated in traditional schooling, but in the kinds of intellectual circumlocutions that leave educators assuming a deficiency.

I first met Gardner several years ago, in the course of researching an article about Lawrence Taylor, the celebrated linebacker of the New York Giants. That Taylor had risen so quickly to greatness could not be explained by athleticism alone; it was also, I was learning, a matter of his mind. Gardner saw in Taylor's case comparisons to musicians and artists, those who process information not in the step-by-step process we commonly see as learning but rather in clusters. The brightest among them — the Taylors, the Picassos, the Casals — in fact process this information so quickly and so efficiently, that their brains are working infinitely faster than the plodders among us, those whom we celebrate for intellectual acuity because they sound so smart when they explain what they do. For the others, learning, and the application of that learning, happens too quickly to be broken down. So we assume that they operate on instinct — they "have a nose for the football," a patronizing way of saying that they are idiot savants.

Gardner, not a football fan but nonetheless struck by Taylor's story, offered a suggestion: Ask him whether he sees the plays in slow motion; ask if he sees them in reverse. "Of course," said Taylor, who innocently assumed that everyone saw things the way he did.

Everyone, of course, does not. Only the exceptional mind — in Lawrence Taylor's case, the football "genius" — processes information so rapidly that it is as if things are proceeding in slow motion for him. Taylor's assumption that everyone shared his vision of the game is much like the way schools and those who run them see children. Surely everyone can learn math and science, if only they apply themselves. Surely every young mind absorbs knowledge the same way.

Gardner's point is that they do not. Moreover, he argues that there are multiple levels of intelligence. And different levels of intelligence, Gardner says, require different means of instruction. Children, he insists, want to learn. Granted there will always be the children in class who resist education, be it for psychological or sociological reasons. But most children want to be engaged. And school does not engage them — and then blames them for being uninspired. "The chances for getting excited in school are very small the way it now works," Gardner says.

The blame does not fall on school alone. It is hard to motivate the child who sees no real reward for his effort, who comes from a home in which the adults around him or her have not benefited materially or emotionally from their schooling, and when those around him tell that school is for chumps. It is wrong, Gardner says, to presuppose that all schools are places where all children can come to learn. But that does not mean those children do not want to learn.

Yet the system endures. It endures because it is easier, because it remains, in the words of Theodore R. Sizer, director of the Coalition of Essential Schools, a "Conspiracy for the Least."

The way school generally works is easier for teachers, and students and parents. It is easier for overburdened, over-worked, underpaid and undervalued teachers because all they have to do is teach one lesson, to all their students, at the same time and leave it to the students to absorb its high-lights. It is easier for parents because in the ritual assessment of the report card they can see a quantifiable analysis of their children's supposedly growing wisdom and feel satisfied that they are being adequately prepared to meet life's challenges. And it is easier for students, who seldom need to take an active part in their own education.

Sizer, who is also chairman of the education department at Brown University, says it best in *Horace's Compromise*, his study on American high schools, when he talks of the unspo-ken compromise between teacher and student: There's a limit to what I can do for you, and so I'll limit what I ask of you.

But school need not be that way. It can be better, and tougher — tougher in that it can become a place not of drift-ing but of purposefulness, where demands are made and expectations high. It can be a place where showing up and staying in your seat is no longer enough to qualify for gradu-ation, but where you will demonstrate that you have mas-tered the knowledge required of you.

The operative word here is *mastery,* a welcome replace-ment for *passing.* In the view of Sizer, and other advocates of wholesale reform, school would be a place where students are expected, with the aid and guidance of teachers, to seek knowledge independently — or with their peers — at their own pace, and in their own way. In the end they will be asked to show they have "mastered" a body of knowledge.

Mastery is not a paper written out of the encyclopedia. Though it can be measured in writing, or in an oral presen-tation, mastery seeks imagination. It requires the capacity to draw inferences from a set of facts. It demands that a student be able to show that he or she is on such intimate terms with a body of knowledge that they can speak of it with the authority of one who truly knows.

Before she ever came to Francis Scott Key Junior High School, and before she ever heard of "active learning," Jill Gaulding understood what it meant to master a subject. When she was in seventh grade her class studied the period of the French Revolution. Rather than assess their knowledge through measuring the accumulation of names and dates, her teacher had the class prepare the artifacts to enlighten an archaeologist about that moment in time. Jill contributed a language.

She gathered information from many sources; and when she sensed that she understood the period so well that she could devise a language for it, she decided that her language would not be spoken, but sung. Jill composed her language along the lines of a musical staff. And then, to demonstrate the depth of her newly-acquired knowledge, she sang the language of her imagination to life.

*   *   *

It is two months since Ms. Gaulding drove the needle into the balloon and introduced The Body Book. She has gone to the art supply store and bought a black folder and paper to fill it. The class has decided on the title, and decided, too, that when their book is done they will give it to the school library.

The Body Book project is supposed to work like this: the class is split into eight groups; each is responsible for learning the workings of one system in the human body: muscular, nervous, skeletal and so on. When they've mastered the material, they will teach the rest of the class what they've learned. They will also add their knowledge to the book, with pictures they draw, quizzes they devise, compositions they write and even cross-word puzzles for their readers.

It is May and the project is not going as Ms. Gaulding had hoped. There have been good moments — students who had seldom shown much interest plunging into their work; each group asking when their turn to lead the class would come. But there are problems. Assignments which Ms. Gaulding thought interesting and perhaps even fun — describe the journey of a hamburger through the digestive system — were, in the rare instances when they are turned in, unimaginative and uninspired. There is only one textbook for her students to use. A second exists, but Ms. Gaulding learns too late that the books are locked away in a storeroom. Where, then, will her students find the information they need to teach themselves so that they can teach others? She does not want to lecture, but wonders whether she has a choice. She would like more give and take in class, but the students do not listen to one another. The end of the term looms and Ms. Gaulding's class must be ready for finals. Her hasty preparation never gave her the chance to experiment in her method and approach before she stepped into a classroom. Now, the necessary trial and error happens before the impatient audience of her students.

The Body Book limps toward completion. The nervous system has yet to be covered. Ms. Gaulding, her classes' interest in The Body Book waning, and time running short, stands in the front of the room, clipboard in hand, prepared to assess group points for after-school detention. Much to her regret, she has become the source not only for knowledge, but for punishment.

Ms. Gaulding asks for a volunteer and finds one in Rashid. There are three tubs of water in the front of the room — hot, cold and tepid. She asks Rashid to place his hands in the hot and cold and then to plunge them into the tepid water. Now, she asks, which hand was hot and which was cold? Rashid is not sure, and Ms. Gaulding explains that Rashid's brain is being told two different things about two different sensations and is not sure what to think.

Today, hoping that her presentation might spark discussion, she launches into a story she knows they will like. Imagine, she says, a terrible car accident. Mr. Barton, the science teacher, is killed. Mr. Ward, the Spanish teacher, needs Mr. Barton's brain to live. Doctors perform the world's first brain transplant. But this is not a heart or kidney. This is a brain. What happens to Mr. Ward when he has Mr. Barton's brain in his head?

Walter gets up. She tells him to sit. Someone else needs to use the bathroom, "the mother fucking bathroom," he says.

Carlos turns from talking to a friend and says, "You can't just rush out and get any organ. It's gotta be a match." Then he asks, "Can you live without a heart? Is there blood in the heart when its transplanted?"

Greg asks, "When blood clots it stops flowing, right?"

Ms. Gaulding, an eye on her target, asks, "When would Mr. Ward no longer be Mr. Ward?"

Carlos lays across two chairs in the back of the room. John rises to follow Ms. Gaulding around the room. Wherever Ms. Gaulding goes, John walks with her and when she stops he stands at her side. He wants Ms. Gaulding to notice his new tee-shirt with "Button Your Fly" across the chest. Ms. Gaulding would like to notice, once. John shadows her.

"You still have your own thoughts," Mildred says. "If you have a different brain you still have to fill it up. When you move a brain you have to start all over."

But what would happen to Mr. Ward if he had Mr. Barton's brain, asks Ms. Gaulding? Would he scream, "Shut your trap!" like Mr. Barton? Would he still be Mr. Ward?

Carlos wants to pass to the bathroom. Ms. Gaulding, knowing his game, tells him no. Carlos, tweaking up the intensity, doubles over in mock pain. John stands next to Ms. Gaulding and chats with a friend as Ms. Gaulding, noting that Travis is talking, deducts behavior points from his team, threatening them with detention.

"It wasn't me," whines Travis.

"Mr. Ward wouldn't know how to get home," says Mildred. "His wife would say, Who are you? He'd say, I'm your husband."

Walter, now seated, asks, "What's the nervous system do for you? It gives you like reflexes?"

Ms. Gaulding, not averse to the digression, asks, "What else does it do?"

Walter looks puzzled.

"It helps your brain function," Sylvester says.

"It helps you move and react to the environment," says Greg.

Walter says, "like if something was to happen to you, your feelings."

"It helps you sense what's going on," says Ms. Gaulding, who stops, again, to issue a warning for detention.

"If you think about it," Greg says in a voice so soft it risks being drowned out, "it's like your nervous system gives you a sense about what you can say or hear."

Mildred says, "Maybe Mr. Barton is too smart to be in Mr. Ward's body."

"Mr. Barton doesn't know Spanish."

"He'd lose his job and his wife."

Greg asks, "What about the different shape of your skull?"

Royann, wiggling her hand, asks, "When you grow up, does your brain grow?"

Sylvester drifts across the room.

"Can it shrink?"

"Does your head get smaller, too?"

"When you get a headache, that's from stress and noise, right?"

Ms. Gaulding explains that headaches are pain from the muscles around the brain. Then she says, "We're not going where we need to go today." There are 12 minutes left in the class. Ms. Gaulding has not yet gotten to the demonstration on neurons. She does not want to limit the instruction on transmitting impulses across the nervous system to the material she has written on the board. But the digressions and interruptions for detention warnings are eating up the period. She tells the class to take out clean sheets of paper and write what she has written on the board about the names and tasks of the neuro-transmitters.

Mildred slams her books and bags onto her desk. The talking grows louder and Ms. Gaulding warns the class that talkers will be placed on detention instantly. Carlos pleads to go the bathroom. Mildred mutters to a friend, "just so I can graduate and get out of this school."

Ms. Gaulding places Victor on detention. Victor has not yet taken off his backpack. He shrugs. She warns Effie to be quiet and Effie says, "I didn't say nothing. I ain't doing no detention."

Travis, too, is down for detention. "That was a warning you gave me."

She quickly calls for three volunteers. John takes his place at her side. Ms. Gaulding wants the three to stand side by side, at arms' length. Each will be a different kind of neuron, transmitting information to the brain. The messages will be transmitted in waves along their arms. "Do a Michael Jackson," someone calls out, to which someone else says, "that's right, if he does a Michael Jackson he goes on detention."

Ms. Gaulding moves along the length of their arms to their outstretched fingers, showing how impulses move from neuron to neuron. She asks, "what does the spinal cord do if it notices heat?" John takes the brain from the plastic body and throws it across the room.

Then from the growing din comes the voice of Royann who asks, "Why can't the sensory neuron do it by itself?" And as the bell rings Ms. Gaulding, still battling, explains that neurons are not capable of sending messages by themselves and need each other's help.

"This," she says, when the class files out, "was almost a medium day."

She can see what happens when they want to know. She hears them call her name and wave their hands madly to catch her eye. She knows that they hate copying information off the board almost as much as she hates writing it. She recognizes that they want to work on their book, to teach the class and show how much they know. But she knows too how much of a struggle the simplest instructions can be, how the slightest distraction can stop them dead, how they know only too well what is coming at the end of the term — another exam which will show how little they know. She cannot battle them and the clock and the "Essential Learning Outcomes" and the district and the administration. She cannot use books she does not know exist and cannot wait for the Teachers Choice catalog supplies to come.

She can sense that she can reach them, that they want to be reached.

Then the bell rings and in the only sustained burst of energy of the day, her students are gone and the mice reappear.

*   *   *

Jean Lythcott believes the reason so many students hate science is because they are smart. "Why go into something," she asks, "where you're going to be beaten over the head?"

Lythcott, a professor at Teachers' College at Columbia University and for many years a science teacher, both laments the decreasing number of American students who drop science courses at the first opportunity — and careers in science years later — and understands their desire. Science education, she explains in her bemused way, has little to do with explaining how the world works, and everything to do with learning the words that are supposed to explain the secrets of the universe. Indeed, science's core components rival math's as the holy grail of the multiple choice test. Science for students now enduring it, and for parents recalling it, means photosynthesis, quantum physics, mitosis, DNA, the Periodic Table of Elements, genus, ganglia, neutrinos, and axons, terms that exist on blackboards and in textbooks seemingly not to illuminate but to terrify. It is reassuring hearing from a science teacher that these words that have so tortured generations of young and decreasingly eager minds, are the scholastic equivalent of art criticism — codewords that sound great but make sense only to a very small circle of friends.

Of course the words have wider meaning. But too often in science education, Lythcott says, they have no context. They appear not as a means of explanation, but as an end in themselves — as in, Quick, define photosynthesis. Better, she argues, to learn about the wondrous relationship between a plant and the sun. The word photosynthesis exists as a useful label. Or at least that is how it should exist. But too often, she says, science education comes down to "I can tell you what an atom has and not what it is."

And yet science education proceeds relentlessly, not only in the material to be covered during the term, but in the goals the nation's schools are supposed to meet. Science, along with math, has emerged as an educational crucible where America will once again take on all those incredibly good students in places like Japan, Germany and Korea. Science is where, by the year 2000, we will once again show what young Americans can do when we set their minds to the task.

The idea of "winning" at science is not new; science education, as it has come to exist, is a Cold War phenomenon. In his book *Restructuring Science Education*, Richard A. Duschl of the University of Pittsburgh School of Education argues that science education is a result of the nation's anxiety in the years after Sputnik, an anxiety that convinced America's leaders that we desperately needed a new generation of scientists. So America set about teaching science for prospective scientists by inculcating them with certain essential truths. Duschl writes that lost in this campaign spearheaded by such groups as the National Science Foundation was that idea that discovery and learning begin not with facts but from theories. Theories are there to be tested, accepted or rejected. It is okay for a theory to be incorrect, to collapse in the face of evidence. But what is not okay is leaving a student out of the process of discovery, so that they have no sense of how an idea came to be, but only what was proven in the end. The student who does not see the process by which explanations evolve is the one who is robbed of the ability to draw inferences based on that knowledge — If a sweater does not generate heat, then the heat must come from the body; if it comes from the body and I wear a sweater on cold days, the sweater must alter the warmth coming from the body, or else I would just wear a tee-shirt.

One of the great ironies in the evolution of post-war science education was a concomitant evolution in the new field of science history. And what scientific historians were discovering just as science education placed a growing weight on fact over theory, was not only that theory lay at the heart of scientific discovery, but that discovery was shaped by the beliefs that a scientist carried with him. This was as true in the knowledge civilizations carried from generation to generation as it is for the student who believes in the heat-producing sweater. Theories do not exist in a vacuum; rather they are examinations of the existing body of knowledge which sometimes show a new way of seeing the world.

From the testing of new theories and from the inferences drawn upon that existing body of knowledge, science found new and often better ways to explain the nature of the world. It proceeded from the understanding that discovery was a messy business in which failure — the theory proven wrong — was a given. And only from failure can learning — understanding — occur, a fact that remains lost on those who have shaped present-day scientific education into a compendium of facts in which students have no sense of the "chain of reasoning," of how we have come to explain the way the world works.

The "tragedy of science education," Duschl writes, is the central belief in "absolute truth." Because from such a premise comes ossification. Nothing new is offered. Nothing new is learned.

Jill Gaulding knew this. She knew that, in the end, for her students to learn she could not proceed strictly along the lines the system laid out for her. There were many elements of the curriculum that Jill liked. Her trouble was with the timetable, the idea that the scientific method was to be taught and presumably mastered in three days.

But systems die hard. Systems make demands that one ignores at one's peril. Only when the system absolved Jill of her responsibility to it, when the ostensible demands of the curriculum were met, would she, the trained scientist, observe that learning can happen in the most unexpected ways.

In the end The Body Book did not become what Jill had hoped it might. At each step of the way, the obstacles, from supplies to the ability to follow instructions, stymied the process. Anxious to see the book handsomely produced, Jill had wanted typed versions of each group's report. But most of her students did not have typewriters. To have typed each report herself would have not allowed her to prepare anything else. And so the project ended — well, but not overwhelmingly so — and soon it was time for final exams.

Jill's eighth graders, like students all over the nation, were wise to the way of school and understood that once finals were over and grades turned in, there was precious little reason for them to bother showing up, or, at the very least, to pay attention to anything she had to say. So Jill, hoping to at last put to the test the theories she had brought with her in the fall, decided not to talk but to show — and then to have them begin the process of becoming scientists. She began with sunflower seeds.

Her students devoured them. So Jill, knowing that experiment days, despite their many perils, still excited them, came to class with Ziploc bags and seeds and began asking questions. She'd gotten the idea for making "germination bags" at the board of education's science training center in Queens. The preparation was simple enough: take beans or seeds or anything that might grow, place it in a bag and change the environment. Place the bag near a window; add water; add salt; see what happens. But rather than fill the bags with dirt, which made observation impossible, the trick was to fill them with paper towels and water, or any of the other substances that tested a student's hypothesis.

Jill came not only with supplies but with questions. On the day she first brought the sunflower seeds to class she realized, just as she was about to enter the building, that the seeds she'd bought — the seeds her students ate — were most likely salted, baked, or treated in a way that made them inert. The students would fill the bags with seeds and nothing would happen. So she ran to a nearby bodega and asked whether there were any other kinds of seeds for sale. The puzzled owner offered bird seeds. Jill took the bag, hurried to class and told the class about the question that had just presented itself. And with that the testing began.

In the course of those three weeks the walls in Jill's room became ever more crowded with germination bags. One student, theorizing that shells were a factor in growth, painstakingly scraped off the seed shells before sealing the bag. Others added food coloring. Still others placed their bags in the closet to measure the impact of light. They came to class on time and sometimes when they were supposed to be in other classes, just to see how their seeds were doing.

They traded insults over the bags, insisting that their seeds were doing better.

"It was purposeful chaos," Jill says. "I had this weird kind of freedom." Liberated, she conducted an experiment of her own. She told her classes that they were her guinea pigs. They took it as a form of flattery that she was thinking of ways to teach the coming year by watching them.

*   *   *

And so it was that she returned in the fall, lugging a large box. She placed the box in the front of the room. The students wanted to know what was in the box. That, she told them, was for them to find out. She did not spill the contents, but rather removed piece after piece, each time asking for hypotheses based upon observation. First she took out an envelope bearing one of the assistant principal's names. Then she took out a balloon. Then came the matches. "They really needed to know," Jill says of her classes' introduction to the scientific method by concluding that what she'd brought to class was a birthday party kit.

Despite her many lessons learned, however, the year was not always an easy one for Jill. Discipline remained a source of almost constant irritation. Motivation would wax and wane, as would interest. The "Essential Learning Outcomes" still loomed. Supplies never quite made their way into her classroom. When she planned to introduce her classes to the metric system, she learned that while there were metric rulers in the building they remained locked away. Left without the tools for instruction, she brought in lengths of string and had the class invent a unit to measure length. They settled on the name of a classmate, Tasheem.

Armed with their string and with a new-found basis for measurement, they scrambled about the room, calculating lengths in Tasheems. And then, just as things seemed to be going so right, Jill saw once again how tenuous the moments of true learning remained.

Two students got into a fight. Fights happened all the time. But this time the principal was walking down the hall. She stormed into the room, and without asking Jill what had happened, seized control and ordered everyone into their seats. They sat at their desks, sullen. Jill could see how angry they were at the kids who started fighting, at the principal and at her. The learning ended before they understood what they were so feverishly trying to master. And in that moment Jill saw yet again daunting obstacles squashing fleeting possibilities. It was all well and good to talk of active learning, or hands-on education, or students proceeding toward mastery at their own pace.

But that concept, marvelous in theory, was too often overwhelmed in practice. So Jill and her eighth graders, joined together in the struggle to know, had to content themselves with moments of discovery that came and went all too quickly, leaving in their wake the bittersweet memory of what learning could be.

3

Never Smile Until Christmas

Tom Super (University of Minnesota, '90)

On THE DAY TOM SUPER WAS FIRED his students cried. This surprised him. He had envisioned smiles from the hardest cases and, from the others, empty eyes.

He knew he was finished the week before when the principal, already upset by the chaos in his fourth grade class, happened by at the very moment a fight was ending with one student holding his hand over an injured eye. She told Tom, "You have one week to shape up." Then she closed the door behind her, once again leaving him alone with thirty children he had already lost.

His final week brought no end to the fighting, the talking back, the wandering about the room, the defiant refusals to follow instructions. Still, Tom waited to speak until everyone was quiet. And it was if he were whispering in the wind. He told the children, "all eyes on the teacher." They looked at him for a moment or so, and then turned away. Tom was left standing at the front of the room, tie loosened, shirt tail slipping from his slacks, and one hand raised to signal silence that never came.

On the day he was fired Tom Super had the flu. "I didn't know what to expect going in that day," he says. "I thought they'd be indifferent." Instead they wrote him little notes that read, "Don't go," and "Don't leave." Even his tormenters were quiet. He had known the class only seven weeks. "I don't think they ever hated me," he says. "I do think they thought I hated them."

But now he told them, "It hasn't worked out for you or for me. I tried my best." Then a community volunteer addressed the class: "You kids have been so out of control you've driven him out." Only later, after he packed the belongings in his Brooklyn apartment and headed west for Los Angeles and his girlfriend, Tanya, did Tom understand why his students had cried: They had failed him; and now he was another person walking out of their lives.

But even with the bittersweet memory of the final day, Tom was haunted by what had happened to him in Brooklyn. That memory would shape the teacher he became, a teacher who did not seem at all like the teacher he thought he might be. Given a second chance he vowed that he would never let another class defeat him. "I made up my mind," he says, "I'm not going to let it slide." Next time he would heed his colleagues' advice: "Never smile until Christmas."

"At the time I didn't have a lot of experience at being a disciplinarian or authoritarian," Tom says. "I guess I wasn't totally prepared for the discipline thing."

*   *   *

He wasn't prepared because no told him. The one comment I heard repeatedly from Teach for America's pioneer corps was that in the course of their eight weeks of preparation at the University of Southern California no one had explained to them what to expect in the classroom. While lecturers spoke about the "philosophy of education," there was, save for the week of student teaching, little if any practical instruction on how to control a room full of children.

Student teaching had left Tom Super with the illusion of control. Because while he taught, there, standing in the corner, was the teacher, whose stern voice and commanding presence kept the class in line. Then, like generations of other first year teachers, he was thrown into the deep end of the pool and told "swim." What Teach for America had accomplished in its first summer of teacher training was to condense into eight weeks the same shortcomings that traditional education schools stretched over four years.

It has been that way for decades — this perception on the part of teachers of teachers that the skills of "classroom management," were points to be picked up as you went along. My father, for many years a New York City school prinicpal and now the headmaster of a well-to-do parochial school, tells the story of his first class, at New York's Westinghouse Vocational High School, in 1949. One day at the end of class, the bell rang and as the students filed toward the door, my father saw that they had covered the entire floor with newspaper they'd been shredding throughout the class. This was their statement about his authority. Because no one in the teacher ed courses he took at City College had bothered telling him what to expect and what to do, and because he had had no student teaching experience, he was left, as most new teachers are, to yell and threaten and pray that they'd listen.

Forty years later, after ten years as a teacher, five as an assistant principal and twenty-five as a principal, my father, when asked about the state of teacher training now and in his day, says, "It's not that we've never found a way to systematically train good teachers. We've never found a way as a nation to train systematically merely competent ones."

His criticism was not of the teachers, who time and again, and with no choice, learned on the job. Rather he faulted the teacher training schools and programs. And in that he was not alone.

"Most teacher education programs are too impotent to make a difference," John I. Goodlad, author of a sweeping study on teacher training, told *The New York Times* in 1990. The chief complaint of those who advocate restructuring teacher education is the gulf between the university and the classroom. Even a year of student teaching, say the critics, does not give teachers-in-training the chance to systematically connect the lessons they're learning in the lecture hall — as they're learning them, not three years later — with classrooms filled with students and their problems, demands and needs.

Teacher training, say the reformers, like the training of physicians, must be two-tiered: the theoretical combined consistently with the practical. It is not enough, they argue, to simply learn on the job, or at the knee of an experienced teacher. It is pointless to learn the rudiments of classroom management, for instance, without first understanding how psychological problems manifest themselves in class.

Without the theoretical training, the reformers say, classroom practice becomes a process in which the ways of the past, and the mistakes of the past, are passed along by classroom teachers who may be skilled at maintaining discipline but who may have not kept abreast of the latest research on, say, levels of intelligence. By the same token, without the practical application of an extended "teaching internship," the theories advanced by professors long removed from whatever time they might have spent in the classroom remain abstract and unrooted.

But even with those reforms teacher training remains a process cursed from the outset. Because unlike the training of doctors, there is no assumption of significance in the task. It is universally accepted that being a doctor is hard work, important work, and that it takes an intelligent person to do it well, or at the very least, to make it through medical school. Not so education. Education is seen as the last best hope for those who couldn't make it anyplace else. Besides, we ask, if teaching were really that hard why would anyone with half a brain do it for such lousy money?

We still regard teaching as something akin to owning a restaurant: Everyone has eaten out and therefore assumes that they know what it takes to own a restaurant. Except that most new restaurants fail, just as most new teachers struggle.

In the case of teaching, everyone has been to school, recalls a sufficient number of lessons and therefore assumes some expertise.

For their part, the corps members also assumed that because they had succeeded at school and liked school they could succeed as teachers and make children like school, too. They were smart. How difficult could it be? Besides, in their hasty preparation they were taught, and later lamented believing, that discipline was a problem solved by an engaging lesson. Terrific. They'd come to class filled with infectious excitement about learning and the children would want to learn. Except that no one told them about the student who in response to a question about fractions replies "fuck you."

Because Teach for America was founded on the belief that smart people could be taught to be teachers in eight weeks, critics charged that the program ended up sustaining that dismissive view of the profession. "We keep thinking of teaching as women's work, as easy work. Everybody can teach. All you have to do is breathe and follow the chapters of the book," says Linda Darling-Hammond, a professor at Columbia University's Teachers College. Teach for America, she argues, "is based on the wrong assumption of what it means to be a teacher: an Ivy League education versus a grasp of human qualities."

Critics like Darling-Hammond do not question the enthusiasm of the teaching corps. Rather they take issue with the assumption that over one summer you can make a teacher who will then be assigned to a classroom filled not with students who will learn despite a new teacher's flaws, but who are most desperately in need of the best teaching. The problem, of course, is that Teach for American exists because many of the best teachers do not wish to teach in those schools. Which means that those already encumbered children become guinea pigs upon whom fledgling teachers learn as they go.

But would more training make the difference? Perhaps, says Tom Super, he would have learned to spot the differences between an "acting out" child and an "attention seeking" child and a "vengeance seeking" child. At the very least he would have learned about the psychological burdens that so many children of poverty bring with them to class, seen the manifestations of those problems in a controlled classroom setting, and observed an experienced teacher's techniques for coping with them.

Lengthening the preparation time, however, assumes that more training makes for better teachers. The evidence suggests that it does not, that for the most part teacher training continues in the same, traditional, predictable and often lifeless vein in which it has proceeded for decades. What a marvelous world the classroom would be if all young teachers were trained at places like Teachers College, or at revamped and revitalized education departments, such as Michigan State's. How much better America's classrooms would be if teaching institutions followed the leads of such schools as the University of Washington and California Polytechnic Institute, which have established formal ties with elementary and secondary schools. There, students maintain an ongoing connection between the lessons of the university and those of the classroom. Year after year, they go back and forth, learning and then observing, studying and applying their studies to real life situations.

But would Tom and the other corps members have been attracted to the program if they were told that their first year would be spent learning, observing and assisting in the classroom, an idea that Darling-Hammond advocates? Tom and his wife Tanya Guttierez (also a corps member) doubted whether many of their colleagues would have been interested in a program that did not promise a speedy path to classrooms of their own. "That's part of the attraction," says Tanya. "Having a classroom. That you can have control of this."

Wendy Kopp, Teach for America's founder and president, understood this. Although she has never taught, she acknowledged that were she offered a place in a program that offered her a classroom after she'd spend a year assisting — and learning — she would demur. For Kopp, too, it is a matter of control: "I would just want to be in charge."

Just as Kopp understood the thinking of those who apply for places in the program, so too did she understand the ways in which her program let them down that first year. "We looked at all the other teacher training programs and asked, 'How can we accomplish this in six weeks?'" she said of the length of training after the first summer institute. "We found it extremely frustrating to live through those institutes."

Frustrating, she explained, because the program replicated so much of what was wrong with teacher training, and so much that is wrong with teaching. The first summer institute was essentially an array of required courses, combined with student teaching. Moreover, while Kopp had envisioned systematic assistance for the corps members — such as mentors — the teachers were often left, as Tom Super was, to fend for themselves.

But that, Kopp said, had changed. A few weeks before the start of the third summer institute, she sat in Teach for America's New York office and explained how things were going to be different.

If the first two groups of corps members complained of "feeling like sheep," as they were led from classroom to classroom where they were force-fed teacher education, now they would essentially be in charge of preparing themselves. The program had prepared guidelines of what it expected its corps members to know after six weeks, and on which they would be evaluated by the teachers who taught them.

They would be asked, for instance, to write about who they expected their students to be: their backgrounds and the range of their abilities. They would be asked to prepare a list of five different teaching strategies, bearing in mind cultural sensitivities as well as the appropriateness of those lessons for the students they'd be teaching. They would be asked to explain what method of discipline they'd use, and what measures of testing and evaluation. They'd be asked how they would involve parents in the life of their classrooms, and to write sample letters of the sort they would send home with their students at the beginning of the term.

Teach for America, in turn, would provide classes and teachers and then leave it to the corps members to decide what they needed to learn. The group would be divided by region so that not only would people in the same geographic areas get to know each other — the better to seek each other out in the course of the school year — but their instructors would be teachers who knew those areas, who knew, for instance, what problems and conditions were specific to the Bronx, or to Inglewood, or to rural Louisiana. At the end of six weeks the corps members would then depart for their new districts, there to learn the dynamics of the schools, the community, and the children.

Interspersed through those first six weeks would be periodic chances to student teach — in two-day blocks after the third, fourth and sixth weeks; five days during the fifth. Their teaching would be evaluated by their instructors.

In addition, Kopp said, Teach for America would ensure that all its corps members had mentor teachers to whom they could turn for help. And there would also be the local Teach for America representative — a teacher, or perhaps a retired administrator who'd be available for consultation. All of this would be accompanied by periodic gatherings of all the corps members in their area, an effort to keep them from feeling the isolation felt by so many teachers, new and experienced.

Not only would corps members be issued clear guidelines for their progress after six weeks, but also for what was expected of them at the end of two years. Those guidelines, Kopp explained, were modeled after those issued by the National Association of State Directors of Teacher Education and Certification.

Kopp read the program for preparing the newest group of corps members: "content sessions," seventy-five minute classes in subjects ranging from elementary mathematics and science, to education psychology and special education. In confronting and adjusting to its flaws and in fashioning a new preparatory course, Teach for America had borrowed the ideas championed by the most progressive educational reformers who believed that the lessons that stuck were not those rammed down students' throats, but those they learned on their own paths to "mastery."

But at the same time I remained discomfited with the emphasis on speed. Granted, the program was rigorous in seeking out the best people. But, bright as they might be, surely no one could be prepared for so arduous and important a job as teaching in so short a time, no matter how well they could display the characteristics of leadership, maturity and flexibility that the program looked for in choosing its corps members. But to what was I comparing Teach for America? To something undeniably better? Or merely to something longer? The problem remained that teachers who had a choice often did not want to teach in the worst schools.

As an example of the kind of attrition rates that exist in inner-city schools, consider the case of Thomas Jefferson High School in Brooklyn, a school in which one student shot and killed two others on the day the mayor was coming to visit — the suspect was said to be afraid of being shot by one of the victims. About half the faculty at Jefferson have temporary licenses of one sort or another, says Freida Homer, an assistant principal. She estimates that at Midwood, a Brooklyn high school in a predominantly white, middle-class neighborhood, almost all of the faculty were regularly licensed. "Our reputation precedes us," she said, "and sets up a psychological wall that people don't want to cross. The trick is to get them into the building."

But too often the problem is that despite the best intentions of the administration the schools remain frightening places that teachers rush to leave for someplace safer. What Teach for America was offering was not merely fresh faces, but people who had applied for the chance to come to those schools. Could they be better trained? Of course. Were they taking places from people with demonstrably better preparation? In most case, no.

In *Ed School*, their "brief for professional education," Geraldine Joncich Clifford and James W. Guthrie, professors of education at Berkeley, argue that if teacher education programs are ever to emerge from the peripheries of the universities where they sit undervalued and, too often, unimportant, the field must take itself and its mission far more seriously. Teacher education must be made not easier, but more rigorous. Clifford and Guthrie advocate the end of undergraduate degrees in education, the implementation of national standards of competence for teachers — with assessment both on paper and in the classroom — and a commitment on the part of education schools and departments to end their long practice of seeking approval from their universities and departmental peers ("see, we're doing things just like you; please think highly of us"), and instead commit themselves to being what they are: professional schools.

By raising the level and the rigor of teacher training, and by raising teacher salaries and standards of performance, Clifford and Guthrie write that the field can go a long way toward achieving the social and academic respectability that it sorely lacks.

Yet when their book was published in 1988 they could still argue that "schools of education are in a weak position to contribute forcefully to the forthcoming challenge of improving quality."

Which, a year later in 1989, still left a great gaping hole into which Wendy Kopp's idea for recruiting and training a new and attractive crop of teacher fit very nicely.

It was not a case of Teach for America having found a new and better way to train teachers. Rather, it had simply found a way to attract top students with a novel approach. Because the sorry truth was that these people were, by and large, not going to consider even two-year careers in teaching unless someone came along with a quick route to classes of their own. If they had been, there would have been no need for a Teach for America. The program, in turn, gave its members an overview of what to do, how to do it, and now thankfully, perhaps a better sense of what to expect. And it promised them people to hold their hands.

Kopp is convinced that no matter how many months or years of training new teachers receive, they are still going to go into their first classroom feeling unprepared. Perhaps. And perhaps with four years of training that rivaled four years of medical school they might not. But that is seldom the case.

I did not think it beyond the realm of possibility to prepare people for the experience of their own classrooms, any more than it was beyond the capacity of medical training to prepare doctors for their first surgery with some assurance that they were not learning as they cut. But because too few teacher training institutes were training teachers well, and because the best students were not choosing to enroll in the best programs, Wendy Kopp was right when she said, "I don't think there's another way to do it." Not if you wanted to get the best people — the people everyone said they wanted.

And so despite the best efforts of both teaching schools and Teach for America, what endures is a system in which each year thousands of first-year teachers like Tom Super are, in essential ways, unprepared. And too often they end up feeling the way Tom felt after his principal told him she was letting him go "for the sake of the children."

"I went every day hoping it would be a good day, and to get through the day," he says. "I didn't really meet failure in school. I got one C in college. I guess my first failure in education was teaching in Brooklyn."

*   *   *

It was an innocent Tom Super who came to P.S. 305 in the decaying Bedford-Stuyvesant section of Brooklyn. It would have been surprising had he come any other way. Most teachers bring to the classroom the memories of how they were taught, and like parents who shudder when they hear themselves using the same admonitions and threats they heard from their parents, and then using them again, so too do new teachers quickly fall into the habit of teaching as their teachers taught them.

Tom brought another memory, and that was of himself as a student. School, as he remembered it, was a place for obedience, raised hands, and many, many A's. Years later he would recall getting into trouble only once — an eighth grade shoving match that escalated into his lone fight ("And it wasn't even my fault."). Tom came to Brooklyn after a childhood in Little Falls, Minnesota, a town north of Minneapolis. He graduated from the University of Minnesota with a degree in journalism. But as graduation approached the newspaper business held ever less appeal. Undecided about his future he applied for a place in Teach for America, hoping that he might find a new path in teaching.

He was, on the surface, all wrong for Brooklyn. Everything about him screamed white bread to children who did not seem very much like children as he remembered them. He was pudgy and blond and, in the context of Brooklyn, cursed with a demeanor that combined gentleness with befuddlement. His tie looked as if someone had used it to yank him across a room. His hair sat in a mop on top of his round face. He used words like "cuss" and "crud." He was, in short, a mark.

*

There is a chemistry in a class that works and you know it the moment you walk in the door. Something is happening between the teacher and students; there is a connection between them, an understanding. The feeling is not defined by silence. Quite the contrary. A class that's clicking is purposefully messy. Hands are raised, as are voices, because the mood of the room is one that says, "I want to be part of this."

The mood is not consistent; there are exciting moments, and there are moments that drag. And yet the class never loses its rhythm, its tempo. Or rather, the teacher and students never lose each other. The easy comparison, of course, is between an entertainer and an audience, except there is one essential flaw: teachers and students do not gather once, for a couple of hours. Rather they are locked away together, day after day, week after week, month after month. To say that a successful teacher is merely a good performer is to dismiss a top trial lawyer as no more than a good talker.

But as exciting, and uplifting, as it is to watch a class that works, so too is it excruciating to observe one that doesn't. The death of the relationship between teacher and students begins with a loss of faith, in that once the students lose the feeling that they are willing to work for the teacher, there is little that teacher can do to win them back. He or she can intimidate them, threaten them, bully them, punish them and make their lives miserable. That teacher can keep the kids in their seats, and too often that is all that is expected of them. But that teacher will never really teach them, not as he or she might have had they not lost the trust and faith and confidence of the students.

It is mid-September, not even a month into the term, and as Mr. Super writes the day's objective on the blackboard — "contractions make two words into one by replacing one or more letters with an apostrophe" — their minds are already elsewhere. Perhaps the mentor he's been promised might have suggested an approach more lively than collectively replacing "I am going to the Mets' game" with "I'm..." But the mentor often has to substitute for other teachers and, though understanding, is seldom available. Maybe by watching the mentor, or having time to observe experienced teachers — and then talk, in an education class, about the lessons drawn from those observations — he might have learned such valuable tips as not answering his own questions.

And not repeating a student's answer, thereby reinforcing in the students' minds the idea that knowledge came not from one another, but only from the teacher. And not leaving the front of the room to put out a brush-fire in the back. He might have learned not to quiet a student by hunkering over the child's desk while the rest of the class seized the moment of his de facto absence to start talking.

These were matters of technique, skills that could be acquired through experience. Knowing them might have made life easier, and survival perhaps possible. Without them he was as helpless as my father had been his first day at Westinghouse Vocational: a soldier armed with a wooden rifle facing a machine gun nest. Watching him was like watching a struggling juggler taking on more and more balls.

"I want your attention, class," Mr. Super announces after first arguing with a student about whether the homework he is turning in was for math or science, and then walking to the back of the room to impose order. "I want those eyes coming up to Mr. Super."

The eyes glance at him, and then turn away.

"I'm still waiting for those eyes to come up front."

In the back of the room two children play with toy cars on their desk. Others fold paper into fans.

Mr. Super tells the class that contractions are very important and asks what letter they'd replace with an apostrophe to make one word of "I am."

Then he says, "Let's wait till we have some of the eyes in the back of the room."

He waits for an answer and hearing none tells them that the letter dropped was 'A.'

It is time for practice worksheets. "As I hand out these workbooks I'll be remembering who was doing work." He comes to Melvin. Melvin is a hard case. Melvin is not wild, or angry, or violent. Instead, when Mr. Super says, "Look at me," Melvin refuses. When he tells Melvin to open his workbook to the right page, Melvin ignores him.

As he leans over Melvin's desk, the other children talk. Some stare off into space.

Mr. Super, regaining his place at the front of the room, says, "I'm talking up here." Two boys start fighting and he stalk to the back of the room. "What's the problem?" he asks. "I'm going to have to move you."

When trouble erupts elsewhere he asks, "What's going on here?" No one answers. But everyone knows.

So too did the administration, which offered its help — when it was not criticizing his bulletin boards and the paper on his classroom floor. The assistant principal came to Tom's room and showed him how to keep the children in line. He stood at the front of the room and ordered the children to sit quietly with their hands folded on their desks. He told Tom, "If they breathe wrong catch them at it," and "make them snap to it." Tom tried to be the "dictator" that the assistant principal told him he had to be. But while the children feared the assistant principal they recognized that there was no reason to fear Tom. So when the assistant principal left the talking resumed, and the hitting, and the strolling.

"What do you do with a kid walking around the room?" Tom later asked. "You send him to the office and they'll send him back and he'll still be walking around the room."

More and more Tom was caught between his need to impose order where none existed and his belief that all that that accomplished was sustaining his children's hatred of school. He did not want to be mean, but sensed that if he was anything but the children would stomp all over him. He wanted them to learn and he wanted them quiet and these did not seem compatible.

"What does 'hard' mean?" he asked. "Being hard on them the whole day — they're numb to it. That's what the school told me they needed. I guess maybe over the year they need it. But they also need to know that there are people who are not just going to be bosses, that you can trust authority, too. You have to be fair. I tried to be fair there.

"But these kids, I don't know. I don't know that they're learning the way they should. Why should they ever trust a teacher? What benefit is it to these kids? They learn they can't trust a teacher because a teacher is out to get them."

In the end they got him, or rather they never found each other. It was if they were speaking different languages, all the while asking for the same things. Tom wanted to be in charge but did not want to be cruel. His students wanted to know who was in charge and did not want to be yelled at. What the assistant principal was telling Tom was not so much to be harsh but not to let the students think he was soft because once they did they'd be lost to him. Of all the many sad things about Tom's seven weeks at P.S. 305 perhaps the saddest was his awareness of just what his students needed — his authority and compassion — and his inability to do anything about it.

"I got seven weeks of the best experience," Tom says. "I wanted to do it right. There was no way I could fail at teaching."

*   *   *

On the last day of class at his new school, Tom stood among the empty desks, triumphant and relieved. Brooklyn had offered a new assignment in the same district. But Tom, despite falling hard and quickly for New York, decided to leave, for Los Angeles, Tanya (whom he married that August), and a new start. He found it in an elementary school not far from the one where he'd student taught, a school he had left only a few months before naively assuming that he was ready.

He was given a class of second graders. He did not wait before laying down the law. The class, despite their age, understood what Mr. Super was about and begged for leniency. Their previous teacher, Mr. Hollenback, was an aging, kindly man who allowed them to do puzzles in class.

"That ended," says Tom. "We were going to get down to work here. They told me, 'We want Mr. Hollenback back. He gave us recess. It was fun.' They just knew I was gonna work 'em."

And that is how it begins. Or how it begins to end. You come to your first class and they eat you up and you vow that it will not happen again. And you learn what you have to learn to make sure that it doesn't. You learn the value of workbooks because even if they're numbingly dull they keep the kids busy and if the kids are busy they are not making trouble for you. The principal does not hear noise in the hallway and that is a good thing. Whatever dreams you might have brought with you to school evaporate and in their place comes a simple desire and that is for order and an uneventful progression toward the end of the day.

Teachers "burn out" so often and for so many reasons that the United Federation of Teachers in New York distributes a handbook to its members explaining how to identify and defeat job-related stress. The teachers who can take no more and quit do so because they are overworked, underpaid, under appreciated and, in the worst cases, under siege. In a 1980 study of teacher burnout the National Education Association reported that each year some fifty thousand high school teachers in America were attacked, and that one in five required hospitalization. Some sixty thousand were robbed. Those who succumb to the stress of their work suffered from such ailments as ulcers, ulcerative colitis, migraine headaches, high blood pressure, skin rashes, asthma, insomnia and Graves Disease.

In explaining the causes of stress among teachers, Alfred S. Alschuler of the University of Massachusetts at Amherst wrote in the NEA study:

"Deadlines, bells, excessive paperwork, inadequate supplies are 'givens' in most schools. Free periods are 'free' in name only. Rest and recuperation must take second place to preparation and grading. In addition to these normal demands, teachers are harassed, more or less, in every class. Student sniping takes many forms: talking, whispering, lip reading, note passing, asking plausible but diverting questions, insulting the teacher, complaining about assignments, pushing, brushing against, touching or shoving or hitting other students, throwing things, walking around to visit other students or to sharpen pencils several times a period, requesting passes, making a veritable symphony of noises. As many as thirty to sixty such incidents each period require the momentary diversion of the teacher's time. When PA announcements, tardy students, and roll-taking are included in this list, typically less than 50 percent of class time is spent on learning during a period in which teachers are expected to teach from bell to bell."

"I think it's the total weight of these disappointments that discourages people," says Susan Moore Johnson, an associate professor at the Harvard Graduate School of Education and the author of *Teachers at Work*, an examination of school as an increasingly difficult workplace. "It may or may not have to do with the broken windows in your classroom, but the broken windows and no textbooks and no desks and too many kids with enormous problems. And kids who are not able to read and with no social service help. And in a system that doesn't allow for change. And in a society that thinks everyone can teach. People who are truly burnt out are people for whom work once had meaning and for whom that meaning has been extracted from the work."

Too often they become the whiner in the teachers' lounge, counting the days till retirement. Or talking about the children as "them." "I think," Johnson says, "we very quickly dismiss people as uncommitted because they've become discouraged and withdrawn from their work."

And yet when those same people are placed in a different kind of setting, one where they no longer feel abandoned, and in which the atmosphere is not one of survival but of possibilities, they can very quickly change. Like their students, teachers do not want to be bored. They do not want to be made to feel badly about themselves. They do not want to spend their days in rooms with crumbling walls and cracked paint, rooms that all but scream "beyond caring."

Yet that is where they remain, stuck with each other in a place where no one wants to be, doing things that no one wants to do, hating one another for their confinement, counting the minutes until the bell rings. In the end all that matters is survival, which for the student means keeping his or her head down, and which for the teacher means keeping them in line.

For the teachers the years of accumulated frustrations and humiliations are best expressed in the final stanza of a poem published in 1976 by the Southwest Iowa Learning Resources Center. The poem was titled "Burnout."

Now I say
Sit down
Be quiet
Read pages 9 to 17

No exciting ideas disturb my sleep.
I haven't had a complaint in over a year.
Nobody seems to care
That I don't care much anymore.

In Brooklyn, Tom says, "they knew that I cared. There was never a problem with caring." The problem was the fighting, the talking, the playing in the closet in the middle of class. The problem was in trying to figure out whether to teach over the talking or to wait for quiet because neither worked. What made it all the more difficult were the moments when he and the class connected. The children got excited when they could work at the blackboard, or when Tom chose one of them to be the closet monitor for the day. They liked when he read stories to them. But then the troubles would start again, not with the whole class but, as is invariably the case, with a handful of children who grabbed the class from him.

At night Tom would go up on the roof of his building and look across New York harbor to the lights of Lower Manhattan. Then, in the morning, he would come back to school and assume his place before thirty children "who weren't kids anymore."

He had wanted to teach, in part, because he enjoyed being with children. But when he got a second chance he decided that however much he enjoyed their company, he was not going to let these children see him smile.

*   *   *

Now, as he packed away the erasers and books, the puzzles and yardsticks that remained from Mr. Hollenback's thirty years of teaching he talked about the children in his second class. Half of them were Mexican immigrants. They were quiet and respectful and, just the same, he made sure that they stayed so busy that there would be no disruptions. "They told me one day I was mean. They told me in New York I was mean and that was supposed to be a compliment."

Tom had prevailed, just as my father had, forty years before him. When I told my father Tom's story, a story he had seen repeated too many times over the years, I asked what had happened to him after his first, brutal year. I wondered whether he had become a taskmaster, a disciplinarian. He said that he tried.

He learned enough of the skills of the job to learn to impose some order. And yes, he did try to assume the role of the hard guy. Except it didn't last. In the end, my father said, he couldn't help but be himself. Instead he learned, as millions before and since have learned, how to adapt, to survive and to avoid losing his humanity in the battle for control of the room. He did not become the elementary teacher whose method of discipline still haunted him: locking children alone in the school's vast darkroom.

I asked because I wondered what the future held for Tom Super, whether Brooklyn would forever harden him and make him into the kind of teacher he never wanted to be.

On the day he returned to his classroom to pack up for the term, Tom first talked about getting tough. And then he talked about the second time he said goodbye to a class.

It was the last day of Tom Super's first year back at school and after lunch the class had a party. The children played Snatch the Bacon and ate ice cream. Then, at 2:45, the bell rang and Tom assumed that everyone would race for the door.

And while many left, several lingered. They hung around, watching him pack, not talking, just staying with him a while longer. Now, as he recalled that afternoon, he talked of the children who wanted so badly for him to make them line monitors, of the girls who giggled at the back of the line, and of the one girl who, on the day she finally scored well on an arithmetic test, approached him after class said, "Mr. Super . . ." before giggling and running nervously away.

When he talked of the coming term he spoke not of discipline but of wanting to concentrate on his second graders' reading comprehension and vocabulary. He was glad he had a break to think of new ways to teach.

Then he thought of the children staying with him after the bell on the last day of school. "You get through a year," he said. "It's sad to see them go."

Words

Vicki McGhee (Yale, '90)

Ms. McGhee's class meets in a trailer filled with words. The trailer, painted barracks tan, sits with all the other trailers in the shrinking playground at Highland Elementary School. Highland is in Inglewood, a city abutting Los Angeles Airport. There are doctors and teachers and homeless people in Inglewood and among them are the poor families, many of whose children attend Highland Elementary, a school so crowded that, like a factory in peak production, it operates year-round, on four overlapping tracks. The state has promised money for permanent classrooms. While the school waits, the classes meet in trailers, fixed into concrete where children used to play.

Ms. McGhee's fourth graders are bombarded with words, and for some of the children the words stick. It is the other children who most concern her, the children for whom words remain mysteries best avoided. Having grown up with words, she struggles to make these children see in them the power and importance she did. Every few weeks she thinks of quitting. She tells herself, "I'm not getting through. I'm wasting my time." Yet she stays. A Buddhist, she finds comfort in meditation. But she remains troubled. She recalls all the words she heard in her home and then thinks of the words the children hear, or do not hear, in theirs. She asks herself, "What made me different?"

She gives her students words to look at and words to hear. There are the words written in the class pledge — "I pledge allegiance to myself to be the best person I know how . . ." — and in the laws of the class: work hard; respect the teacher; respect classmates. There are words in the simile flip-books, on the synonym murals, and in the books stacked in the library in the back of the room.

The library is a green rug surrounded by short book cases filled with books like *Sounder, The Right Stuff, A Tale of Two Cities,* and *The World Book Encyclopedia.* In the good moments, children sit with their backs pressed to the library wall, leafing through the books. Some bring memo pads to the library and when they come to a word they don't know, they open the thick, green dictionary, look it up and write it down as they mouth the new word.

It is quiet in the library until the hiccups begin. Or the make-believe hiccups. Someone calls someone else, "stoopid." Ms. McGhee, her voice a stern monotone, calls out "five - four - three - two - one," and on one the children still talking risk losing recess.

She wants her students to hear their words, too, like the words they've written in their letters. The class has read "The Talking Eggs," the story of two sisters, good Blanche and mean Rose, who are living with their nasty mother "at the tail end of bad luck" when they meet a magical old woman. Blanche runs away to the city. For homework last night the children wrote letters that Blanche might have written to her mother and sister when she got to the city.

Deirdre goes first. She has written that when she got to the city she found the old woman hungry, thirsty and begging. She took her in. The old woman wanted to help with the cleaning but she, Blanche, would not let her. The old woman lives with her in a house with a new TV. She gives the old woman a name, Delaroni. A beautician comes to do the old woman's hair. "Get rid of your nasty attitude," Deirdre writes in Blanche's voice. "Don't be selfish and mean. Act humble, nice and calm. Understand when people make mistakes. P.S. The reason I'm in the city and you're not is because both of you are despicable."

The class applauds. It is John's turn. John has made up an address and a zip code. He writes that the home he imagines for Blanche and the old woman is a mansion with a butler and maid and pools, indoor and out. Then Alila, who reads with her arms ramrod straight in front of her, reads her letter: "Rose, I hate you. You make me sick. And the old woman doesn't like you either. I call her momma. We wear train-trail dresses. I hate you. I hate you. I hate you. I'll send you money, maybe. You need not be negative."

Now it is William's turn. "Somebody took mine," he says, searching his desk, fooling no one. "I can't find it. All the junk in my desk. I can't find it."

William pours out more excuses. And when he is done it is as if a spell is broken and no one else wants to read their words.

At recess, Ms. McGhee says "I like to learn. I'm good at school. Therefore it shouldn't be hard to be a teacher. It was a very naive feeling."

*   *   *

My parents, both educators, conducted an unscientific study several years ago about words. My father, whose parochial school attracts families of some means, and my mother, a teacher at an East Harlem alternative school, watched and listened as their respective first graders began telling stories.

My mother's students lept ahead. They told bold, graphic stories about the things they saw. I remember visiting her class one day and hearing a long and detailed account of a man's fall from a tenement roof. "He didn't jump," said another student, interrupting. "He was pushed." The story teller, insisting the man was not pushed, proceeded to describe the way his lifeless head looked on the sidewalk.

The stories my father's first graders told were trivial in comparison — stories of summer trips and visits with grandma and going to the museum.

And then, slowly and inexorably, the gulf began closing. My father's children started catching up. My mother's children, despite the power of their stories, stood still. By the end of the year my father's children had long passed them by. The stories they told, while lacking in drama, were nonetheless filled with words — far more words than my mother's children could draw upon. My parents had anticipated this. And though the results were predictable they were nonetheless disheartening and troubling.

My parents knew that it was just a matter of time before the advantages of my father's children's growing up eclipsed the story-telling abilities of my mother's children. They recognized, too, that these advantages were not a matter of wealth or privilege or race. It was something far simpler: the ability of children to impose order upon and make sense of their ever-larger worlds by absorbing more and more words.

My father's children heard more words and were encouraged to use them. When they asked questions they heard words in the replies, words like, "Yes, that is a bus. A green bus. Can you see the big, green bus?" Too often, my mother's children asked questions to which they heard terse replies, like "Yes" and "No" with no elaboration.

I mentioned this experiment to Vicki McGhee, whose thoughts turned to home — her's and her students'.

Willie and Emogene McGhee are talkers and encouraged their children to be talkers, too. "I talked with my parents," Vicki says. "We would talk about what they had done at their jobs and I would talk about what I had done at school." Emogene McGhee worked on an assembly line, inspecting ball bearings. Because it was the kind of job that offered little in the way of conversation, Vicki says, her mother instead talked about her work with and speeches for the United Auto Workers. Willie McGhee, a sergeant in the army reserve, did not necessarily share his wife's views about organized labor, but Vicki recalls how his views softened in the course of all the talking over dinner. So central was conversation in Vicki's growing up that the one time she got in trouble in school was in fourth grade when she brought home a report card filled with A's, except for the U — unsatisfactory — in conduct: She was talking too much in class. Her parents grounded her. In class she learned the value of respectful silence. At home she continued talking.

Willie McGhee often took Vicki with him to work. He was an administrator at an army reserve office, a position that allowed his eager daughter the chance not only to learn the names of all the ranks and classifications, but their respective pay scales. This gave them something else to talk about: "Dad, what rank are you?" Vicki's father took her to lunch and when he was busy one of the men he worked with did. The men knew that Vicki was a talker and knew that lunch also meant conversation, especially if she was selling candy for school. They talked, Vicki says, "about the world." In the summer she visited her grandmother in Chicago. Together they took trips to Niagara Falls, Wisconsin, Florida and Arkansas, where Emogene McGhee had grown up. "All my family," Vicki says, "are talkers."

Willie McGhee also taught his daughter to write checks and balance an account, skills she applied at the age of eleven when she calculated that her father would be better off retiring than continuing to work. "His big thing was that you might not find someone who is going to support you so you better be able to do things for yourself," Vicki says. On every notebook she ever brought to school, her father wrote across the front "THINK." Vicki says, "He was telling me, 'You're capable of thinking, so do it.'"

The McGhees lived in Roselle, New Jersey, a working class town in which blacks and whites stayed on their respective sides of the dividing line of Ninth Avenue. In 1973, however, Roselle became part of a school desegregation plan. Though many white families left, Vicki's was a generation that entered schools no longer defined by racial composition.

She started school already reading, a fact not lost upon her first grade teacher, Sally Weil, who considered placing her in second grade. Though she dropped the idea after talking with Vicki's parents about the impact on Vicki's making friends, Weil remembered Vicki and when she was in third grade allowed her to come back to her class to tutor.

"She just let me go," Vicki says. "She'd say, 'here's what this person needs. Teach him.'" Weil made Vicki feel trusted and responsible, and that was how Vicki wanted to make her students feel when she became a teacher. But while Sally Weil succeeded with Vicki, Vicki, in her lowest moments, would come home from school and tell herself, "I can't be the kind of teacher I had."

These were teachers whom Vicki saw as people who cared not only about their students' progress in class, but also their development as people. "They exposed me to so many ideas, to careers and literature — all those kinds of things." Vicki did not lose touch with her teachers, and when she graduated from Yale, Sally Weil was there to watch.

Vicki did not grow up thinking of Yale. "In Roselle it wasn't a question of ability," she says. "For some people it was a question of reach and how high their dreams were. I didn't think people from Roselle couldn't go to Harvard or Yale. It wasn't something that was pushed."

What was pushed, at least in the McGhee family, was college. Vicki knew she was going to college because when she was five years old her brother Dwight left for Xavier, a black college in New Orleans whose emphasis on math and science has helped debunk the myth that black students cannot excel in those subjects. "When I went to kindergarten that was already the standard in my five-year-old mind."

The Ivy League was not. Perhaps if Abraham Clark High School had been the kind of school rigorous enough to hold her daughter's interest, Emogene McGhee might never have pushed Vicki to go elsewhere. "I was bored," Vicki says. So at her mother's urging she applied for and won a scholarship to Kent Place, a nearby private school that boasted not only that all its students went on to college but that they went to the best schools.

She was one of five black students in her class of fifty. "And that was a large number," Vicki says, comparing hers to classes with one or two black students. "When I first went there I was really scared. I had done well in school. I could compete with seniors when I was in ninth grade. But I assumed I wasn't going to do well because all these white kids were going to do better than me. My only defense was to work. Hard."

Her teachers, too, doubted her ability to keep up, sentiments they expressed loudly enough for the school custodian to overhear. He mentioned that to Willie McGhee, who, talker that he was, used to chat with him when he brought Vicki to school. Later, one teacher, perhaps not recognizing how revealing her statement was, told Willie how surprised she was when Vicki got the only A on a test. She went on to explain that as a result she made the next test even tougher, assuming that Vicki would fail, just like everyone else did. Except that Vicki again got an A. "Surely," Vicki says, mocking the teacher, "I could not be doing that well."

That she was was the result of an uncomplicated formula. "To do well in life I needed to do well in school," she says. "It was something my parents always told me."

And then reinforced with words, both spoken and written. As a child she could think of no gift greater than sports equipment. But at home she read. She was not beaten over the head with the classics. Rather she read books like *Shogun*, *Roots*, and *Taipan*. Her parents did subscribe to the Great Books series, and the volumes filled the bookcases in the back of the house they'd built. When she was old enough to get a library card, Vicki paid a weekly visit to the children's section, returning with a stack. Later she and her mother exchanged Harlequin romances and Stephen King novels. She'd stop at a delicatessen to pick up lunch and buy the local paper, *The Elizabeth Daily Journal,* as well as *The National Enquirer* and the *National Star.* What television the family watched was limited to news and the occasional sit-com. Vicki says, "I always saw my mother reading."

She imagines that Deirdre does, too, because when Deirdre writes she fills page after page. Deirdre's mother talks to her daughters, Vicki reasons, just as Kimberly and John's mother talks to them. She hears it when a visitor comes to class to talk about health and Kimberly barrages her with the kinds of technically sophisticated questions that could only come from the daughter of a nurse who shared her world with her children. "You could tell her mother talked with her about what she did," Vicki says. Of other mothers and fathers she is not so sure.

It is not that their children are slow in comparison, but rather that the relatively limited number of words they use describe a world view filled primarily with TV and Nintendo. "Our kids are very passive," Vicki says, echoing what her classmate Ho Chang and the other corps members were saying about their classes. "And some of that passivity comes from TV. TV is a very passive activity. Words are thrown at you and all that's asked of you is to receive them."

She thinks of these parents on open school night, when five show up — this compared to twenty-five parents of the thirty students in her elementary school class. At Highland it is always the same ones. Deirdre's mother comes. She listens as Vicki tells her how well her daughter is doing, and as soon she hears even the slightest suggestion says, "I know she can be doing better. I'll work with her." Luis's mother comes, too, even though she speaks little English. She wants to know how well he is doing. Hugo's mother wants to know that he is behaving and Vicki has learned that she must be careful in discussing Hugo's behavior because his mother does not tolerate disobedience.

Then, Vicki says, "there are the parents who will believe that for weeks on end a child doesn't have homework. A lot of times the kids are raising themselves. It's amazing that they make it to school. They wake themselves. They make breakfast on their own. Their parents are either without money for food, or have $100 for a pair of sneakers. A lot of them don't realize why school is important to them."

In class these children look at her with eyes that retain little. Or they yell and scream and hit — anything, she now sees, to get her to notice them. And while she understands their need she will not tolerate its expression. Of all her difficult moments, Vicki says, the worst came during recess, a few weeks into her first term. The children were playing kick ball when one child accused another of cheating. She was the referee and so instantly became the target of the cheated child's rage. He started kicking dirt at her. She watched in disbelief. "You are eleven years old," she told him. "I am a teacher. I am an adult."

She had majored in Middle Eastern Studies at Yale, before she decided that she wanted to be a doctor. By her senior year, still making up for all the science she had not taken, she wanted time off. Like her classmate Ho Chang, and all the other seniors at Yale, she found in her mailbox a flyer about Teach for America. That she was black, she learned, made her an even more desirable candidate.

The program intrigued her, for it offered what seemed not only a respite from the rigors of school, but a chance to think of people other than herself. "I felt much of my previous experience was self-centered," she says. "I had always loved school. I wanted to instill that love in kids."

That summer Vicki learned how to prepare a lesson, and how to map one out, in seven points, from the review and motivational moment of the "anticipatory set," to writing the day's "objective" on the board, to the "guided practice" that followed her instruction, through the quick "check for understanding" that preceded the class' "independent practice." She learned, too, how difficult it could be to teach "amazing lessons" in each of the seven subjects she taught each day, and that sometimes the best approaches came to her in a burst of inspiration the night before — like the math lesson she taught with the principal observing, the one in which she asked the class to make a menu at McDonald's for the entire grade so that the principal could pay with one check. Vicki was pleased with that lesson, pleased that she had avoided the trap of teaching math by getting her students to multiply big numbers that meant nothing to them. She'd also learned, in her brief summer of teacher education, that the lessons that stuck were the ones that spoke to students about their lives. So too was it with the words that stuck, the words the students clung to because they helped describe their worlds.

Vicki had student-taught in Los Angeles and felt she had a sense of what to expect. Because of the year-round schedule, she started in late August, taking over the class of a retiring teacher named Mr. Henderson.

On her first day she explained the class rules, just as she'd been advised to do. Then she told the class that they could expect to work hard. She had been warned about the perils of losing the children in the early moments. So she scheduled a fifty-question math test. And while that subdued her students for a while, it did not seem to shake them as much as she'd expected.

"Mr. Henderson let us do this," objected one student said when she recited the rules.

"I'm not Mr. Henderson," replied Vicki.

"I wish Mr. Henderson was back."

Vicki thought, "I cannot believe a ten-year-old child would say that to me."

She was just beginning to learn.

*   *   *

Vicki taught math, science, history, and all the while she saw that what she had to teach was reading because without words none of the other lessons made sense. "Reading," she said, "entails so much. I could spend all day teaching reading."

Not only did she not have that luxury, but she found herself trying to bring comfort with words to a class whose abilities ranged from grade level to that of first graders. The school and district were similarly aware of the great numbers of children who were falling ever further from literacy. And so, before the term began, the district decided to discard the familiar methods of teaching reading and writing and adopt a program called Whole Language.

Whole Language advocates a simple idea: that it is foolish to continue teaching writing and reading and speaking independently of one another, because they are bound together. Reading can no more exist in a vacuum of its own than can writing. Rather, they flow from one to the next, all the while connected by words and by ideas. It is no longer enough to teach, say, prepositions. Prepositions, taken alone, are abstractions. But learning about prepositions as they exist in literature — not a paragraph for drilling purposes, but real stories with themes and plots — brings them to life. Prepositions are a means of expression, a tool that gives the child who knows how to use it the power to convey to many people the ideas that live in his or her head.

Writing, and reading, are in the view of Whole Language advocates just that: the expression and dissemination of ideas, students' ideas. The students read. They write about what they read. Then they build upon what they read and write by drawing upon those lessons to write what they want to say. This story telling, however, is not an exercise in stream of consciousness. Instead it is modeled after the rigorous business of professional writing — re-writing and re-writing again until "a piece" is ready to be "published." In the instance of "The Talking Eggs," for instance, Vicki, in a traditional lesson, would have likely asked the students not to tell the story from a new perspective, but would have asked questions designed to test their comprehension: Who was the good sister, Rose or Blanche?

Whole Language proponents argue that with that kind of teaching, students ultimately gained little; little, that is, that added to their command and fluency with words. Because until the words become their words, express what they want to say, they remain empty sounds that, like so much else in school, reside only in the mouth of the teacher, or on the printed page. The Whole Language advocates also argue against teaching children to write by first inculcating them with the rules for good writing: the rules come not because they were required, but because children learn that they can help them make their points.

So gone from Highland Elementary were the basal readers and their accompanying workbooks, the Dick and Janes that had ushered generations of children into the lifeless practice of writing and reading in school. In their place came a new set of guidelines, taped to the classroom wall, guidelines from inception to publication.

Instead of teaching by category — Cause and Effect Week, for instance — the new approach was to teach by themes, themes that would spark the student's ideas, which, in turn, would trigger their search for more and more words to explain all the things they wanted to say. The themes were designed not to make things easier, but to stretch the students, demand that they think big: Face the Truth; Achieving

One's Dreams; Accepting Challenges; Sharing. These were the new lenses through which the students were to see the stories they read. Because through them, the reasoning went, the students would apply the lessons of those stories to their lives and their ideas.

The first time I saw this happen was in my mother's classroom, long before I met Vicki McGhee. My mother was then teaching a combination of kindergarten and first graders who were failing at writing. But now they sat at their desks, telling the sometimes frightening stories about the things they saw around them. Having heard I was a writer, they wanted to know whether I "published" my own stories and "drew my own pictures." Then, after they'd finished telling their stories out loud, they began writing their first drafts.

I looked over their shoulders and saw writing like I'd never seen before. I saw letters that represented words. I saw long words, misspelled. I saw words running across the page in no particular order. And yet, as the students explained what they were doing, that muddle transformed itself into something far closer to the writing that I knew as an adult than was the writing I'd known as a child. Here was writing filled not with repetition of the teacher's, or the basal reader's, ideas, but with ideas that belonged to the authors.

The words became not the end but the means. And that, in the teaching of writing, is a revolutionary concept. Bear in mind that the teaching of writing as so many Americans grew up knowing it, was, in good measure, an outgrowth of the desire of the nation's elite educators to see that the new crop of students who started coming to places like Harvard in the late nineteenth century might have suitable skills in composition. In her book, *Growing Up Writing*, Arlene Silberman recounts how in the 1870s educators such as Harvard president Charles W. Eliot found themselves all but overrun with a new sort of student who was not the son of a prominent family, but of a man of sudden wealth. These students were, in the view of such hide-bound educators, unprepared as writers for places like Harvard. And because the best schools did not want to be in the business of training all its incoming students in the basics of good and correct writing, they began requiring of those applicants essays that would display their competence in written English. It was left to their high schools to prepare them.

The rules, long existent in the world of a privileged and well-educated few, were now spread throughout the nation's network of schools. Composition became the order of the day and would remain so for generations. The reasoning behind it went something like this: you could not write until you knew how to write and you could not know how to write until you knew the rules for writing. Therefore, you first had to learn the rules. Then you could write. Of course, as millions of Americans were to learn, the definition of writing as an embodiment of those precious rules served to all but choke any spark of creativity out of the work that appeared in so many composition books.

Silberman writes of her own painful experience with trying to commit that most seditious educational crime: being different. Lamenting the death of so many young imaginations — as evidenced by the comfort in the assigned topic: "On my summer vacation we went to Grandpa Ed's fishing camp . . ." — she recounts how, as a high school sophomore, she wrote an essay criticizing *The House of Seven Gables*. "Standing in front of the room," she wrote, "and displaying my paper with a scarlet F on it for the entire class to see, my teacher thundered my name. 'Young lady, who are you to criticize Nathaniel Hawthorne? It would be like my criticizing God.'"

That day in my mother's class one of her children wrote an upside down E for a word I cannot remember. Was that inverted E enough to get his point across? Of course not. Which meant that he couldn't just leave it there on the page. He had to find the word, write it out in the familiar form, or risk letting his idea evaporate like disappearing ink. With the search and subsequent mastery of that word as a beginning, that student could then start thinking of how the word fit into a sentence. And then in a paragraph. And then in the larger context of his story, a story that was not suitable for publication until he had found a way to take the ideas expressed in his "rough draft" and put them in a form and context that made sense to those who might read them.

In the beginning, at the most important moment in the creative process, that student's mind was not encumbered by abstract terms like modifier and sentence fragment. That was for later. That was for his revisions. But before that moment of completion, there was a word, a word that existed in his head, and which he might not be able to say. He, together with his teacher, sounded out the word, and then wrote it out, and soon that word, because it served his greater purpose became his. Forever.

My mother, however, worked at an advantage, for her students did not come to class burdened by three previous years of learning to read and write. Of course, some of Vicki's students, the students like Deirdre, flourished within the system, as some students always had. But even among her fourth graders there remained those who still could not sound out words. Or if they could sound out the words, could not retain the main points of a story. Or if they could both say the words and remember the story, could not complete a written paragraph.

Untested, she faced a task that would try the most skillful and experienced teacher: starting over again, with a class filled with widely different abilities, in learning how to think and execute the essential and ongoing lessons of reading and writing. And too often she was doing it alone, because the people who'd helped her, and who helped students like Deirdre — the parents — were either overworked, or uninterested in expanding the world of their children through words.

*   *   *

Vicki McGhee's world, too, was being transformed, but in ways she had not envisioned. If her success at school had taught her one lesson, it was about the power of an individual to exercise control over their lives. "School is easy in that you're in charge," she said. "It's up to you whether you're going to do your paper or not. In the classroom you're in charge. But there are other factors, like the thirty kids." Teaching, after all, was about what others might do at her instruction. Not that she could make her children do things they did not wish to do, much as she tried. "I can't demand that anyone learn. I can invite. I can teach. But I cannot force them."

And now she was being asked to teach in a way far more demanding of a teacher. No longer was it enough to have students take turns reading out loud and then fill in the answers in their workbooks. Now, as she walked along the rows of desks, she had to adjust to each student's needs and pace. Though she dressed casually in slacks, sweaters and black studded boots, she maintained an almost dispassionate air. "I learned," she would say, "that I can be very authoritative."

When one especially angry boy named Terence lost his temper she sat with him for half an hour and said, "You have a really bad temper and you need to control it because being a young black man with a temper like that means there are three places you can end up. You know where Inglewood Cemetery is. You know about gangs and you know about prison. You can end up in all three."

But more troubling than the anger and the back talk — "I wasn't talking to you;" "You were looking at me!" — was the air of defeat that her students carried with them. "Sometimes the kids don't want to think," she said one afternoon, sitting in an empty classroom. "Sometimes they want you to do it for them. They say, 'Tell me how to do it.' I tell them, `You're the one who said I can't. Not me.' For some kids I don't think it really matters."

Like Ho Chang, she tried to prompt them. When they did not do their homework she told them that that indifference would likely mean a future no better than a life spent working at McDonald's — "and," she said, "let me show you how you can't live on that salary."

When that didn't work she tried guilt. She told them, "Slaves were not allowed to read and write because then they'd know things and they'd do things. They died so you could go to school for free."

Yet, she says, "The wonder at that statement did not change their habits."

Vicki knew enough about her students' lives to know who was being raised by a grandmother and who lived with both mother and father. She quickly learned which parents were interested in school and which ones would respond indifferently when she called to report a problem with their child. But it was not until William and Chris asked her to take them to the beach that she learned how distant many of her children were from the world to which words might lead them.

Though they'd grown up so close to the Pacific Ocean, Chris had been to the beach once before; William had never gone. Chris, short and skinny, sat in the front of the room, fidgeting in his chair, calling out answers, interrupting when someone was recounting a portion of a story and left something out. William was husky and filled with excuses for work that never seemed to get done.

Vicki could imagine few things as dull as sitting in the sand, doing nothing. So she took them to Venice Beach, her favorite, where the menagerie of body builders, roller blade dancers, souvenir vendors, and street entertainers — not just guitarists but gymnasts who built human pyramids — would give them something to look at, and talk about.

Chris and William wanted to eat pizza. They wanted to rent roller skates. She did everything the boys wanted to do. They wanted to go into the ocean, too, but as they stepped into the water they got scared and took her hands and would not let go. After they'd dried off, they sat with their teacher on the sand. "They wanted to know," Vicki said, "that I wanted to take the time out to be with them."

But for her the enduring memory of that day was of William trying to roller skate. While Chris was daring and sure, William was fearful. Vicki was not going to let his fear stop him.

"Try this," she told him as he struggled with his skates. "I'll be there to catch you."

*   *   *

In the weeks, months and year that followed that afternoon at the beach, Vicki came to know her students better: talking with them from time to time during lunch, responding as vaguely as she could when they peppered her with questions about her life outside of school ("Do you like Mr. Shaw?"). She was more forthcoming when they asked,"Did you like school? Did you like to read?"

She also grew in confidence as a teacher, even as her education about life in the classroom reinforced her belief in just how difficult the work was. By her second year there were tests she might have felt compelled to give which she now overlooked. Yet the key to motivating her students to learn with the fervor that she had had as a child continued to elude her.

So much of what she had to do seemed to work at cross purposes. She wanted her students to be respectful enough of each other to work together, but at the same time to be

confident to learn on their own. She devised an in-class men-
toring system in which the faster readers helped the slower
ones. When they were done with their work for the period,
the students knew that they would be free to go to the library
in the back of the room and read. That time was a privilege
to be earned. And it pleased Vicki to see that her students
saw a connection between their effort and the reward of time
to read whatever they liked.

She brought in pizza at lunch for the students who
scored well on tests. She brought little gifts and offered five
extra minutes of recess, each time making the rewards harder to earn. She cut the time on the fifty-question math test
from ten minutes, down to eight. And the students, seeing
that they could finish the test in less and less time, told her
to cut it even more, because they began to see what they
could do.

She had given up her attempts to motivate by preach-
ing, sensing that it did no good. Instead she offered her students a view that, she quickly saw, was novel to them, a view
much like the one she learned as a child. She'd tell them,
"Listen, if you don't get a good education, whose fault is it?
It's no one's fault except your own because you are in
charge."

At the same time, however, Vicki understood how easy it
was to slip into despair, even for someone who'd grown up
believing in that message. Each time she thought of quitting
she meditated and chanted. And in those moments of reflec-
tion, she says, she saw "that here was this obstacle in my life
and instead of trying to overcome it I was trying to run from
it. The more I looked at my kids the more I saw myself."

She returned to class resolved not to quit, and also not
to let her students quit either. She did this not by making
things easier, but by pushing them to see what they could do
when they were forced to. "Every person is responsible for
everything that happens in their life," she says. "Even when
we cannot control an external event we can control our reac-

tion to it. These kids are smart and they know a lot and they can do a lot. But they're further handicapped not by circumstances but by their reaction to their circumstances. Some of it is babyness and some of it is lack of confidence. But I made them sink or swim because I know they can swim."

She recalled a math lesson in which each group of students had to make six geometric shapes out of construction paper. They told her they couldn't. They whined that they didn't know how. Only Terence, with whom she'd been so direct about learning to master his temper, pushed ahead. The others gathered at her desk, asking for help. She refused. She told them that they had to do it themselves.

So they went back to their tables and took their scissors and paper and tape and surprised themselves, but not her, with their ability to do what she'd asked. When they were done they said, "Ms. McGhee that was easy."

But then, with the next challenge, they were back at her desk, pleading. Vicki wondered how much of that message of personal responsibility was really getting through. As the term progressed she sensed that at the very least they were remembering enough to repeat her words and gestures to the principal when she sent them to the office.

They remained the best barometer of her progress. If she was teaching poorly she knew it immediately because she could see it in their eyes. And when she was on she could see them perk up and respond, both the quick ones and the ones who struggled.

*   *   *

It is on just such a day, in the week of the worst rain and flooding that Los Angeles had suffered in years, that Ms. McGhee's class is reading a West African story, "Why the Mosquito Buzzes in People's Ears." The story, like so many of the other stories read by this class, and by classes across the district, is a sophisticated story that challenged students to think about the way they saw the world. In pedagogical terms, it is a cause and effect story. Ms. McGhee, aware of the wide range in abilities that still exist in her class, wants everyone to come away from the story with a clear understanding of the logic of telling a story, of the order and progression that makes it understandable to everyone.

To do that, the class begins by reading. Then they write. And then they consider what they read and wrote so they can see what tools, what words and combinations of words, the author can call upon to bring the story to life. And though this involves repetition it is repetition of a different sort. Because here it exists not as a series of meaningless words, repeated over and over, but words that come in a story, a story that expresses ideas.

"Why the Mosquito Buzzes in People's Ears" is a fable that begins when a mosquito whispers a lie in an iguana's ear, who whispers the same lie to a python. The lie spreads from animal to animal until it ends in the death of an ocelot. The rest of the animals punish the mosquito by vowing never again to listen to him. The mosquito is doomed to whispering in ears, and being swatted away.

The class has written the story out in scenes — much like a movie story board — and has written captions for the scenes. Then they trade each other's scene cards, arranging them in a suitable order and re-writing the ending into any they want.

They work quietly. The elements of the story spread out before them, they can begin imposing their own sense of order, creating a chain of events that lead to the ending in their imaginations. They are using the power that words possess to make sense of the world. That they are being challenged to do it themselves means that they cannot simply repeat what the teacher, or book, told them about the progression of events and time. They have to do it themselves.

Ms. McGhee, boots clicking on the linoleum, walks among them — past Rose, who always finishes so quickly that she'll have a hand up, asking what she might do next; past Morris, who struggles to understand the stories he hears; past LeShan who cannot write a sentence. She calls for their attention. It is time to work together, to reinforce the lessons of the story, and the scenes, and the new endings.

Ms. McGhee hands out worksheets that pose this problem: Sally, a slow walker, got to school late. But she did not tell her teacher the truth about why she was late.

"What did she do?" Ms. McGhee asks.

"She told a lie," someone replies.

"Close," says Ms. McGhee.

"She makes up a story."

"But what happens?" she asks. "What went wrong with the story?"

Hands shoot up. "Her cause and effect was wrong."

Ms. McGhee says, "Let's put her story back together."

First, on their worksheets, they review with Ms. McGhee's prompting, the logical progression of tardy Sally's excuse. Ms. McGhee begins the thought, and together, reading from the page, the class fills in the effect.

"Because the rooster was in the way, the cars couldn't move . . ." and so on until Sally explains that because the street was filled with people, the buses were full and because the buses were full she had to walk and because she had to walk she was late.

Now it is up to the class to use their own words to complete even the most foolish sounding idea. It starts with a silly cause: "The boy spilled pink paint."

Rodney offers a fragmentary effect. "Couldn't go to school," he said.

"Is that a sentence?" asks Ms. McGhee.

"No."

"If you say 'I'm getting ready to give a cause' what word do you need to connect your thought?"

"So?"

"So," repeats Ms. McGhee. "'So I couldn't go to

school . . .' This word is really important because it helps us connect the two thoughts."

Someone offers another. "So the boy went skinny dipping."

"That's original," says Ms. McGhee.

"So I had a party because my parents were at work."

"So it was a holiday."

"So he became a pink boy."

"So the floor filled with paint."

"So now he can paint his body."

"So the paint came out of the can on his sister's shoes."

They go on like that for the rest of the period. In the end, Ms. McGhee offers an effect: "Morris got an A on his spelling test."

Morris, seeking a cause, goes first. "Because I got all the answers right."

Someone else says, "Because he studied."

And someone else says, "Because he cheated."

"But Morris would never do that," says Ms. McGhee.

"Because," says one of Morris' classmates, "I helped him."

5

No Man's Land

Jane Martinez (Georgetown, '90)

Pᴜʙʟɪᴄ Sᴄʜᴏᴏʟ 115 sits on a street blanketed in shadow. The street runs perpendicular to the commercial strip along St. Nicholas Avenue. But once you turn the corner and leave the butcher shops, the discount furniture and linoleum stores, the bodegas and Cuban restaurants, once you leave the noise from speakers outside the lay-away plan clothing stores and the sock and glove peddlers and turn onto 177th street, silence descends. The street is like most side streets in Washington Heights, filled with soot-stained apartment buildings with courtyards where children are no longer allowed to play. Young men stand on the corners or in the half light or cruise by slowly in cars booming merengue music over sound systems built for concert halls. P.S. 115 sits in the middle of the street, a fortress walled off by a stone facade cut and chiseled a lifetime ago.

Jane Martinez' kindergarten children come to school late in the morning for half a day. They come dressed in navy blue school sweaters. The girls wear dresses, and the boys slacks and ties. They work themselves out of their heavy coats which they hang on hooks and then take their seats and wait to begin.

There is so much to look at in Ms. Martinez' room. There are pictures of fish on the walls with the days of the week written in Spanish and English. There are flower cut-outs on the windows that the children colored in. Everyday there are games where you count to ten in English and Spanish and games where you call knees, hands and arms in English. Sometimes Ms. Martinez shows how to make things, like the cards the class made for Father's Day. Ms. Martinez wrote out the words, "I love you Daddy" on the board. Everyone rushed to the front to copy them down.

The children bring pieces of their home to class. They bring stories, stories that unsettle Ms. Martinez because the children tell them so casually. She hears how Mommy's boyfriend beat up Mommy, or how Daddy is in jail or that Daddy is dead because somebody shot him. She hears about drug-addicted uncles and a new boyfriend for Mommy who has moved into the apartment with everyone else. "I have three daddies," a boy told her. "My real daddy, my mommy's boyfriend and my grandfather."

Ms. Martinez does not always want to hear. And then the mothers come to her. They tell her how they cannot go on because they are alone with two children and they work by day and go to school by night and only by going to school can they do anything for their children. She meets the mothers at parent-teacher conferences or when they are called to school, like the mother who was asked to explain why her child has been absent for days. The mother assumed that the child's father was true to his word when he promised he'd bring the girl to school when she went to work. She meets the grandmothers, too, the ones who raise the children because the mothers are drug addicts, like the crack addicted mother of three who believes she may have found God. The children tell Jane, "My mommy lives someplace else" as if they were telling her what they watch on TV.

"I want to scream from the top of a building," she says. "I'm sick of the grime and the filth. It would be one thing if I was not from that background . . ."

So she runs. She leaves school and the silence of 177th street for the clamor of St. Nicholas Avenue. She descends the subway station stairs, waits for the elevator and then for the train and within minutes is home, two miles away, in the New York of Columbia University and the Bank Street College of Education and private schools. She returns to a neighborhood filled with bookstores and cafes and Italian and French restaurants, and also restaurants with names like La Casita that serve the kind of food that she insists her mother makes far better.

She thinks of the photographs the children bring for her to see, like the picture one of them brought of her family at the baby shower before her sister was born. Jane Martinez studied the faces of the father and the mother. She knew the mother as a heavy, tired woman with many children. But in this picture she looked young "— and she looked so happy."

But Jane sees happiness only in the children, and even then the happiness is tempered by asthmatic coughs, learning disabilities, and the fatigue of sleep deprivation. She hears from the teachers of the older children about the rage that comes when Daddy disappears and a new daddy appears and then the new daddy disappears and the children are sent to live with grandmother. Or the rage that begins when Daddy dies and Mommy needs to go back to the Dominican Republic and then decides that they must come back to New York but maybe it would be best if the children lived with relatives for a while. Or when Mommy is so tired because she is alone and must work and study and the apartment still has mice and no heat.

Jane thinks often of the mothers. It is not just that the mothers are twenty-three, Jane's age. It is that she could have been one of them. For Washington Heights is where Jane Martinez grew up and where, at a young age, she left for a world filled with people whose lives seemed like the lives she watched on "The Brady Bunch." Her parents and siblings still live here, in a world her parents shielded her from, and from which they sent her away.

When Jane told her younger brother that she was planning to come back to teach after graduating from Georgetown he warned her about overcompensating for leaving. "Don't come back for you," he said. "Come back for them."

"But at least I'm back," Jane told him, not knowing that coming back would bring her not to the world of her youth, but to a place she barely recognized.

"I feel like I'm part of that community," she says. "And yet I don't feel I'm part of it. I'm in no-man's land. I don't fit in anywhere."

*   *   *

Ten years ago Jane Martinez left the cloistered world of her immigrant parents' apartment and traveled south, to a Catholic prep school on Park Avenue where wealthy parents had been sending their children for generations. Jane won her scholarship to Loyola School, a great stone monument of a school, because for years life after school meant not other children in the courtyard but hours at the library, and because she wanted a nun named Sister Yliana to notice her.

She had not excelled in school until third grade. By then her parents had taken her out of public school and placed her in a Catholic school where Jane learned an early and lasting lesson about class: that "public school" was a pejorative term used by children whose education had always been private and who had been brought up believing that any other kind of schooling was suspect. Jane also learned that if you are dark-skinned and come from a home where Spanish is spoken — even as your parents are trying to learn English — teachers will often not expect much from you. In third grade, however, two things happened to Jane: she was placed in an accelerated math class, which spurred her to work harder than she ever had; and she was taught by the first in a succession of nuns, who did not see her color and home as limits.

Tall and skinny, Jane learned, too, that her place in school was not with the boys. Instead, she became one of the smart kids and found a haven in the library. The library provided not only a safe place but an endless source of books that she could take home to her room. Closing the door behind her, Jane lost herself in Nancy Drew and Grimm's Fairy Tales. "Going into my room, and closing the door, would grant me escape from anything that had to be faced at home," she wrote in a story about her growing up. "Everything from doing chores, to listening to my parents argue could be blocked out by entering my new worlds."

She caused her parents few problems. She complied when they imposed their strict rules for a good girl from a Catholic home: no dating; no hanging out. Once a week her mother came to her school to work as a teacher's aide. A seamstress, Jane's mother later went back to school, first to learn English and then to study nursing. She became a nurses' aide and eventually a hospital nurse. Her father first worked as a busboy. He learned English at night and learned to type and later, to become a restaurant pastry chef. Years later, when she was waitressing in college, Jane would meet the newly arrived busboys from El Salvador and Nicaragua and think with sadness of her father, beginning life in America the same way.

But years before college there was Sister Yliana, who changed her life. Sister Yliana first approached her in seventh grade with what seemed like an insulting proposal: summer school. Sister Yliana's view of summer school, however, was not remedial, but accelerated. Together with two other students in whom she saw promise, Sister Yliana offered a summer of rigorous study to prepare them for applying for private school scholarships. Sister Yliana's private academy was a nine-to-three, five-day-a-week intensive course, concentrating on literature and ninth grade math. Joining Jane was her best friend, Michelle.

Where Jane was studious and obedient, Michelle was a problem. Michelle fought with her parents and hung out with the wrong people and Sister Yliana, who'd been a missionary in Peru, saw her and not Jane as the one who most needed guidance. And though Jane now understands how she and Michelle differed, at the time she wanted "to be number one with Sister Yliana." So Jane pushed herself in school. She scored well on the standardized tests. She worked to make Sister Yliana look at her. And though Sister Yliana never stopped watching Michelle, her presence nonetheless gave Jane a mission, a reason to push more than she ever had, and perhaps more than she ever would.

Jane now speaks of school with regret. This is not to say she did not enjoy it, but rather that aside from her time with Sister Yliana she never felt the impulse to excel. School came easily for Jane. So too did rewards. Perhaps, she says, they came too easily. Perhaps because she came from an "under-privileged" background, the people who accepted her into the more prosperous America demanded little. She is haunted by the memory of what those private school interviewers really thought of her and abilities. She wonders whether her test scores, so high compared to her classmates in Washington Heights, might have paled alongside those of students from middle and upper class homes. Given license to glide through school, she did. Given the chance to assimilate, she seized it.

At Loyola, where out of 198 students only four were of color — among them Jane and Michelle — Jane's looks were a novelty that brought her sudden popularity. So too did her origins, but up to a point. People were curious about where she came from, but Jane sensed that their curiosity was limited. Wanting them to think well of her, she did as they did, and acted as they acted. She became a cheerleader. She went to all the basketball games and afterward went out for pizza.

At night she hung out with her new friends in Central Park. She smoked. She dated. All of this brought her into conflict with her parents who, despite her protestations that she was not wasting her time with neighborhood kids, saw no distinction between the idleness of the rich and that of the poor.

Washington Heights increasingly became a place to return to eat and sleep, and an inconvenient one at that, with the long commute and the inevitable arguments. No longer wishing to be part of a neighborhood that she believed offered her nothing, Jane so immersed herself in the world of Park Avenue that while she often visited her new friends in their homes she never invited them to hers. She did not want them to see how she lived.

She was beginning to see the changes in Washington Heights, like the knocks on the door of the drug addicts mistaking her parents' home for that of the newly arrived dealers next door. As much as she tried to distance herself from Washington Heights she could not escape the trip home at the end of the day and the inevitable comparisons with the homes of her new and privileged friends. "I never thought of myself as poor," Jane says. Until she went to Loyola it had not occurred to her that the homes she saw on shows like "Happy Days" were different than her home. "It's very painful coming to the realization that you're deluding yourself," she says. I thought, 'I'm just like them.'"

Georgetown only confirmed the gulf. But it did not end her desire for assimilation. It just left her confused. "I was a mediocre student at Georgetown at best, and it was not because the material was difficult," she wrote years later. "People had always been telling me how wonderful it was that I had gotten scholarships to all these private schools. That because I was a minority, I was set. Well, I began to believe it. Despite the myth that minority students had to work that much harder to keep up, I realized that because of the low expectations set by the system, it was OK not to do my best, as long as I kept up, kept my foot inside the door. I figured as long as I did not get expelled, and graduated in the Spring of 1990, I would be fine; I would finally be that success that everyone liked to talk about. That's exactly what I did."

A New York law firm offered her a job as a paralegal. She thought seriously of taking it. But at the same time Teach for America had begun recruiting. Jane applied, and was accepted, somehow knowing, before she was ever told, that she would be assigned to District 6 in Washington Heights.

She knew that teaching bi-lingual kindergarten would disappoint her parents, who both feared for her safety and bemoaned her return to the neighborhood they so much wanted her to leave. But Jane sensed that Washington Heights held an answer to the quandary that had plagued her since she first left for Loyola. In embracing a new world, Jane could never quite put the old one behind her. She saw herself as others saw her: as a black woman from a poor neighborhood who had somehow managed to break away. But she was not at all sure how to view herself by herself. She was left straddling both lives, which meant that she did not feel truly at home in either.

Perhaps, she reasoned, by returning to Washington Heights she might make her world clearer. And though by coming back she would fulfill Sister Yliana's admonition that those whom she helped leave should one day return to assist others, she was driven as much by compassion as she was by the need to discover herself.

Her brother issued his warning. Her parents asked her to reconsider. But the job held too much promise for Jane to pass up. What she did not know, because she had been away for so long, was that a new generation of children was growing up in Washington Heights, a generation born into a world of death and fear and definition for normalcy that in no way corresponded to the rigid definition of her parents. At ages five and six they came to school with burdens in their hearts. Their pain and scars would leave Jane at once trying to embrace them, while at the same time trying to cover her ears and hurry away.

*   *   *

Geography curses Washington Heights, as does urban planning. The neighborhood spreads across the western portion of upper Manhattan and includes three expressways and the George Washington Bridge. Washington Heights is a commuter's paradise, easy to reach, easy to leave, and that has helped make it the prime narcotics distribution center for the City of New York.

People come from miles around to buy cocaine, and its cheap derivative crack, in Washington Heights. They come from downtown, from the Westchester suburbs, from New Jersey, and, on Friday nights, they drive in from Connecticut. The police in the beleaguered 34th Precinct thought they could cut down on the interstate drug traffic by working with the DEA to impound cars from the caravans that came over the bridge and clogged the streets in front of the dealing centers. But the drug buyers and out-of-state dealers parked their cars on the Jersey side of the bridge and took the bus across. When the Fort Lee police towed their cars the buyers elected to car pool.

Washington Heights has always been an immigrant neighborhood and like most immigrant neighborhood its face has changed often. What was an Irish and German Jewish neighborhood has, in the past generation, become predominantly Dominican. The Dominicans began coming in the 1950s. Mostly it was women who came to work in the city's garment industry. They did not necessarily intend to stay. But many did and many more came, especially in the past ten years, when the population of Washington Heights virtually doubled to 300,000 from perhaps 175,000. The housing stock remained the same and soon families were living with other families in apartments intended for couples.

It is hard now to imagine that in the early 1980s, young white professionals were looking at Washington Heights as the cutting edge of the urban frontier, with its old and spacious apartments that could be had for a song. Those who came and did not soon flee now dare not go to the street to hail a cab after dark, but instead call livery services that pick them up at the front door. They are the lucky ones because their buildings have guards in Plexiglas booths, and because they can leave. Everyone else is trapped. Because to venture out at night in Washington Heights is to risk walking between two young men who are angry at each other over a drug deal gone sour, or a woman, or a slight to their pride, all of which result in a quick exchange of bullets. The killings are followed by a story in the morning papers about yet another good and decent citizen of Washington Heights shot in the temple by a fourteen-year-old trying to collect on a drug sale debt with the considerable muscle of a nine-millimeter handgun.

Death is so common in this, the city's murder capital, that most every morning brings a new, temporary shrine to the front steps of an apartment building where the newly deceased was gunned down. The police here are on the average the youngest and least experienced in the city. Quickly inured, they talk of the neighborhood with a practiced, sardonic air, which dissolves into sorrow and confusion when they describe the sight of a group of school children coming upon a body so recently dead that smoke still rose from the wound in its head. The students stepped around the body, noted the gray ooze flowing, and walked inside to school.

History in Washington Heights is divided into two eras: before crack, and after. Crack came in the mid-1980s, which is when so many more people came, too. Before crack, says Pablo de la Torres, who has been a police officer here for twenty years, kids got in trouble for breaking windows. Before crack a standard for suitable behavior was what teenagers did or did not do on "school nights." But "school nights" is an anachronism, a throw-back to an era when school mattered even a little bit. But in a neighborhood which has among the lowest reading scores in the city, where four out of every ten children live in a house headed by a single mother, and where each year two thousand out of the four thousand students at the local high school, George Washington, drop out, the idea of a "school night" has all the resonance of the anti-drug slogan "Just Say No."

"School nights" here are spent making fifty dollars for buzzing-in customers for the drug dealers upstairs. That's the kind of money the little kids make. It is the older kids, the ten and eleven year-olds, who are the $500-a-week look-outs and couriers. De la Torres, who has watched enrollment in a favorite project — the Boy Scouts — drop from five thousand to eight hundred as the birthrate approached double that of any other Manhattan neighborhood, still visits schools to lecture about the perils of drugs. But the exercise has become so meaningless that his display case of paraphernalia is covered with a thin layer of dust. The kindergarten children can tell him what a standard crack vial sells for, and can also quote the price of a "jumbo."

"They were born into a drug culture," he says. "They see the drug trade as normal. Ten years ago they knew drug dealers were bad."

*   *   *

Jane's best friend at P.S. 115 is Anne Barnshaw. Anne, who also came through Teach for America, had grown up in Wheaton, Illinois and graduated from the University of Illinois. Jane admired her, although sometimes she laughed at Anne's reactions to what in Washington Heights was commonplace, like the day a mouse appeared in her classroom and Anne gathered up her students and led them down the hall in search of the janitor. A mouse was nothing new to

Jane, who also recalled the appalled look in the eyes of a teacher she accompanied to the apartment of a fourth grader being held back. The apartment was the cramped, two-bedroom home of a mother and three children; in short, a Washington Heights apartment that looked no different than the apartments Jane knew growing up.

Still, in Anne Jane saw a teacher who plunged into her assignment. The walls in her room were filled with the results of creative projects and when Jane visited her she would look at what Anne had prepared and her students had done and say, "I could be teaching them a lot more and I'm not."

Jane wanted her students to feel good about coming to school. But while Anne took those feelings and turned them into a desire to learn, Jane measured success by making her students feel good about themselves.

"I like the fact that these kids like me, that I'm making a difference," Jane said one morning before class as she sat in Anne's room.

"How do you know you're making a difference?" Anne asked.

"That they'll look back and say, 'I loved kindergarten,'" said Jane. "That the parents say, 'You're teaching them so much.'"

The week before, when she once again felt overwhelmed hearing the painful stories of her children's homes, Anne sought the advice of the school's guidance counselor, Nancy Schmidt. Schmidt reminded her of the perils of thinking too far into her children's futures. "Teach them and love them one day at a time," she told Anne.

Anne, conceding that she was perhaps too idealistic, and cautious of imposing upon her students a view of life shaped in a childhood in Wheaton, nonetheless found herself worrying about the children and wondering about their mothers. She had learned to recognize not only the signs of abuse — the black eye the child swears came in an accidental fall — but the art of deception that young children perfected to avoid the belt. "They don't know why they're not supposed to lie," Jane told her.

The children played with the truth and said whatever had to be said to avoid painful consequences the moment when their mothers came to see Anne and asked the question they always asked: "How did he behave?" The children knew that lying was bad, or at least that is what they said. But if the consequences of honesty was a beating, they saw no virtue in coming clean. And so the truth became a flexible concept, just like the idea of daddy and home. The rough justice, she also learned, was too often accompanied by what appeared to be either benign neglect or indifference. Anne told Jane about one mother whose child lost his glasses and who, despite her repeated reminders that the child could not see, took a month before getting him a new pair.

But then, like Jane, she would hear from the mothers about the dreams they had for their children, dreams of college and good homes and lives far from Washington Heights. If they had, at the age of twenty-five, abandoned such dreams for themselves, they still believed in them for their children. And that, Anne learned, was why they did not tolerate disobedience in school. That is why the mothers, and the fathers and the grandmothers, reminded Anne and Jane, "You just tell me when he gets out of line."

It was not an absence of love Anne and Jane spoke of that morning. It was something far more complex. It was about being transplanted at a young age from the villages of the Dominican Republic into the chaos of Washington Heights. It was coming from a home where food was abundant — it grew all around — and the air clean and warm, and where people walked slowly, to a place where strangers rushed past you on the crowded streets and shoved their way through the supermarket aisles. In winter it was easy to spot the children who'd just arrived because even on the coldest days they wore tee-shirts. They'd come from a place where the school windows were always open. Now they lived in big, dark buildings and learned very quickly that it was not safe to go out. In Washington Heights it was said that it took three or four years to adjust to life in America. But that adjustment did not occur in a vacuum. It came amidst the late-night pop of gunfire, and the not very gentle persuasion of the drug dealers.

"A lot of these parents are kids," Jane said. "They're living hand to mouth."

For a long time Jane wanted the mothers to think well of her, to accept her as part of Washington Heights. "The fear I had all along was the fear of being rejected by these people," she said. Yet that longing for approval by the people with whom she'd grown up was tempered by her own disapproval of their world. Jane questioned the values of mothers whose money appeared to be spent on new and brassy outfits on St. Nicholas Avenue. She spoke disparagingly of families that, in her view, were not really families; families where the concepts of fidelity and responsibility were, at best, casually applied. When a boy told her about how much he liked his mother's new boyfriend, she thought, "he should be talking about Mommy and Daddy."

But that, she realized, was her increasingly conservative view of the world, not necessarily theirs. It was, more and more, the view of her parents. But even they confused her now. For with two teenagers and a daughter in her twenties, Jane's parents were also the parents of a four-year-old girl and a boy who was five. It was her youngest son whom Jane's mother worried most about, because the street devoured boys so quickly. And Jane, who admitted to wanting to "remove herself" from the world of Washington Heights, saw its new perils afflicting not only her students but also her siblings.

"I feel like I don't want the responsibility to comment on her choices," she says of her mother. "I resent that my parents have two little kids and that four years from now what happens to them will be my fault."

*

In class, however, the outside world temporarily recedes. In class she is in charge and the children, despite their being at an age that could test a new teacher, offered her no resistance.

"Come here Christine. Talk to me," Ms. Martinez says to a returning student after her morning talk with Anne. "I missed you." She sees that Giovanni is wearing his new school sweater and says, "When did you get your uniform? It looks very nice." Giovanni smiles an embarrassed smile.

The children take their places and Ms. Martinez asks, "Did you guys have homework?"

The children take their homework from the book bags, and place their assignments on their desks so that Ms. Martinez can see how they've written their names. She walks between the clusters of desks, bending low to look at their work. The children pull on their faces and chew on felt markers as she compliments one and reminds another to "zip your mouth." Christine sings to herself. Ms. Martinez tells her it was not the time for singing. She reminds another girl to take off her coat. She reminds her every day because every day the girl sits in a her coat long after everyone else hangs theirs up.

It is time to come to the front of the room, one by one, and gather on the rug. The children begin counting to ten, in English and Spanish. Louisa, usually bubbly, sulks. Ms. Martinez asks "Are you sad about something." Louisa says nothing. Crystal begins dozing, as she did each afternoon.

"Are you tired?" Ms. Martinez asks. "Were you sleeping before you came to school? Is that why you were late?" Crystal nods.

Ms. Martinez asks the class what they did during the weekend. They tell her they watched TV and played video games. Together they sound out the letters of the alphabet. "I'm really impressed," says Ms. Martinez.

Christine begins drifting. She is looking around the room when Ms. Martinez calls to her. "I'm over here," she says, trying to bring Christine back to class.

*   *   *

There are 1,800 children in P.S. 115 and one guidance counselor, Nancy Schmidt, who this morning saw a seventh grader whose been absent for a month because his mother cannot get him to go to school, a second grader whom she suspects is drinking with his alcoholic grandmother, and a third grader who was mistakenly placed in a special education class. The third grader returned to the Dominican Republic and has not yet come back to school.

He might. Parents will enroll their children in P.S. 115 and keep them in school until Christmas, when they return to the Dominican Republic to see relatives. Sometimes the children return to school in January and sometimes they come back in March. "Many children," Schmidt said, "have never been to school at all."

Those who do come are not necessarily ready to learn. The reasons vary; but their cumulative effect produces acute cases of burn-out among the people whose job it is to come into their homes and lives. Schmidt is the exception. A legal secretary until she broke her arm in a company softball game, she went back to school, earned a degree in special education, taught in schools that did not even have chalk, and moved into guidance.

Now she meets children kept off the school bus because their parents did not know they had to be inoculated against tuberculosis. Or the boy with 20/70 vision whose father balked at getting him glasses because he insisted his son's low reading score was a result of stupidity. Or the girl whose father took her from her drug-addicted mother in the Dominican Republic and brought her to New York where she met two sisters she did not know existed. Or the children whose mothers keep them at home to care for the younger children. Or the third grader whom she believes is trying to starve himself to death.

In her office is a rack filled with brochures: "Being Me is Great;" "Good Health;" "You Don't Want to Hurt Your Child." But the saddest thing in this big room with the institutional green walls and hissing radiator is the mural. It is an artist's rendering of a make-believe town. All the houses are single-family homes. The stores have names like Toy Town, Rogers Supermarket and Annie's Bakery. *The Wild Pony* is showing at the movie theater. Children play outside Morgan Elementary School. The doors of the public library are open. The sky is clear and the day sunny and in the background are fields and hills. People are walking to work or to the shops, except for one woman who stands with her hands on her hips, watching a house burn down. She is the only one who notices.

"Why did you drag her by the hair?" Schmidt asks the chubby girl whose teacher sent her to the office. This is not the first time the girl has erupted in class. This time she was angry at a friend who is pretty and whom everyone likes. "How do you feel when she gets away with everything and gets all the attention?"

"I get very angry," says the girl.

The girl wears tight pants and a sweat shirt that read "Ducky Mooners." The clothes belonged to her older, thinner sister. "Your mom says you wear your sister's clothes," Schmidt says. "Some of those clothes are too tight for you."

She asks, "Why do you get angry so much?"

The girl fights back tears.

"Why?"

"I don't know."

The girl lives with her mother and two sisters. Her older sister is pretty. Her mother goes to school. Schmidt has encouraged the girl to go to an after-school program where she can learn about nutrition. She asks the girl whether she had gone. The girl says she had not and Schmidt asks why.

"My mother says they're all black people there."

Schmidt sighs. "What does your mom say to you?"

"She says I'm gonna blow up."

"Does she put you on a diet?"

"She says I should go on a diet."

Schmidt asks, "Who does your hair?" The girl points to herself.

"Does your mom ever help?"

The girl shakes her head no.

In P.S. 115 there is nothing unusual about the kind of rage that makes a child grab another child by the hair and drag her across the room. Today Nancy Schmidt will climb the school's five flights of stairs thirty-two times to attend to variations on this anger, anger that comes from being young and sure that you are worthless and undeserving of love.

From time to time Aurea Martinez visited the school and together she and Nancy Schmidt commiserated about the things they saw and the stories they heard. Martinez, who taught parents to teach other parents about how to use birth control and how to better rear their children, worked in the district schools as part of Columbia University's Center for Population Study and Health.

She had been working in Washington Heights for twenty years and her weariness was coupled with rage at having seen too many children who hadn't a clue where they belonged in the world. She told the story of a girl whose parents left her behind in the Dominican Republic when they left for New York with her older brother. While the girl lived with her grandmother, her mother cleaned houses and her father worked nights. When her grandmother died her aunt took her in and her uncle began abusing her. After ten years her parents had saved enough money to send for her.

She came to their home not the child they remembered but as a bitter adolescent who looked like she was eighteen. She joined her parents and brother in an illegally rented basement apartment where she was warned not to turn on the television at night because people might see the light and report them. "She despised them," Aurea Martinez said of the girl whose story was like that of so many other children whose parents, poor and overwhelmed, had little time left over for tending to the emotional well-being of their children. The parents themselves felt worthless. They would tell Martinez how they longed for home because at least at home there was food to eat and decent air to breathe. Now, they told her, people looked at them "like they brought the garbage with them." Their children, meanwhile, were closeted away in apartment blocks that the newly arrived called bird cages, with windows that looked like so many holes from which to fly away.

The beleaguered mother of the teenaged girl told Aurea Martinez, "I want my girl to be innocent." She was anything but. The girl stopped going to school. The last time Martinez saw her she too had become a mother.

Aurea Martinez wanted to offer these children hope. But the encouraging talk rang hollow. She knew it and they knew it. When the children got older she talked to them of the virtues of education and the good things that come to those who stay in school. They told her, "C'mon Mrs. Martinez. You know I'm not going anywhere."

She told them, "You'll do good."

"Where?" they replied. "All I have to do is go downstairs and make a thousand dollars. Tell me I'm ever gonna get a job making a thousand dollars a week. Ever."

Aurea Martinez listened and asked herself, "Why am I lying to them? There's no way these kids will get to a good college. From first grade they're not prepared."

*   *   *

No one in this country has done more to show what poverty can do to the psyche of a child than James Comer, director of the Yale University Child Study Center. Twenty years ago Comer, a psychiatrist and associate dean of the Yale Medical School, launched an experiment at two New Haven schools that would forever change the way we think of the needs poor children carry with them into the classroom. Comer focused on the family, or rather the essential things families did not, or could not, provide their children. The result, he believed, was that children came to school so burdened by sadness and fear, by all the psychological damage of growing up in homes that did not function as families, that they were in no way prepared to learn.

Given the failure of the families, Comer sought a substitute. He found it in school. If a free and open society could not justifiably impose itself upon a family in its home, he wrote, it could offer the alternative of school. Comer schools — there are now over one hundred across the country — concentrate not only upon learning, but also upon the child's mind. In addition to involving parents in the life of the schools, and educators in managing those schools, each school has a team of mental health workers who assist in evaluation and counseling.

The program, however, is not about psychotherapy for children. Early on Comer saw that little good would come of delving into the lives of the children in the schools, that teachers and parents who were committed to the program would not be at all pleased at the idea of family life being pored over by the newly-arrived experts at school. Instead, the counselors, together with the teachers and administrators, focussed on the manifestations of troubles, the acting out, the tantrums, the chronic passivity.

In his book *School Power*, Comer tells the story of one violent child, the kind of child whose behavior would have led to the all-too-familiar progression of punishment: banishment from the classroom; detention; suspension; dismissal.

Rather than confirm what the child already believed — that he was undeserving of love and attention — the boy sat down with his teacher, principal, and school social worker. They talked with him. They told him that they knew he was not happy and that his unhappiness was at the heart of his behavior and that as much as they wanted him to be in the school they could not tolerate his violent outbursts. The key was that they wanted him. And so together they would work out a plan — that he would agree to — that would help him get back into his class. The responsibility for its working, they explained, was his.

The child was not sent to the teacher across the hall or made to sit in kindergarten until he "learned" to behave. Instead he began by spending an hour a day with the principal, helping. Soon he began spending a second hour with a special education teacher who worked with him to overcome a learning disability. Gradually he was eased back into the classroom. The child was told what was expected of him. And he was shown, again and again, that people in authority cared very much what happened to him. When he slipped, he did not incur their wrath, but, as any parent knows, something far more potent: disappointment. He was letting them down. And so, given the responsibility for his own fate, he didn't.

The point was that the health care professionals and the educators recognized what this child was saying through his actions: They heard him crying for help, just as they would hear other children making the same plea in different, unacceptable ways.

The school was addressing a simple need: the need to feel wanted and worthwhile. Comer recognized that too many poor children did not feel this way about themselves, that they lived in homes where people had no time for them, did not listen to them and too often gave very little indication, if any, that they wanted them. But they were going to feel wanted in school. Because only if they felt that way, only if they felt a little good about themselves, were they going to be receptive to learning.

"Often the question of whether teacher, principal, and others cared about him or her was what the testing, acting-up behavior was about in the first place," Comer wrote in *School Power.* "'Do you love me, even though I can't read as well as Mary? Do you think I am important even though my clothes are not as nice as John's? Am I a nice person even though my father has an embarrassing drinking problem?' Such questions are rarely asked directly. With young children the behavior is the question. Yelling at them, punishing them, and ignoring them without addressing the underlying questions can be a statement: 'I don't like you, you stupid, poor, person from a troubled family!'"

*   *   *

On St. Nicholas Avenue the vendors have set boards on top of milk crates and on top of the boards rows of double-A batteries and cassette tapes. A woman peddled socks and panty hose from a overstuffed plastic bag. Men and women milled about the sealed entrance to the defunct Ensign Bank. Bushel baskets of yucca, green bananas and batata spilled onto the sidewalk in front of a bodega. Jane Martinez emerged from the subway and looked around her. Sometimes, she said, she enjoyed the walk because it reminded her of walking along Dyckman Street in the Washington Heights of her youth. "Sometimes," she said, "I want to tell people here, 'Get a clue.'" She shook her head and hurried to the shadows of 177th Street and school.

She was midway through her second year of teaching and her past and present felt no more resolved than they were before she returned. She remained at once saddened by the poverty and despair she saw, and contemptuous of the parents whose interests did not seem to include the welfare of their children. Though she wanted these mothers to know that she was one of them, it seemed that when they wanted to confide they turned not to her, but to her paraprofessional who seemed so much more accessible.

It would have been easier for Jane had she returned to Washington Heights with the conflict between her past and present lives gone. But because it was not, every moment Jane spent in Washington Heights served as a reminder of the precariousness of her life. No matter how far she had come, she felt, she was still part of this mean, dispiriting place.

"I still feel that sense of betrayal," Jane said. "I feel a part of you. And not a part of you."

So Jane stayed, committed to the simple idea that if she could give her children one thing it was a memory of a year in which school was a place where the teacher liked you and hugged you and told you in a hundred different ways that you were wanted. Perhaps she could have taught them more. Perhaps she could have increased their vocabulary and facility with numbers. But despite those shortcomings, she gave them something that mattered far more. She gave them a new place where they were at home.

Today Ms. Martinez and her children stand in a circle on the rug in front of the room. The children look up at Ms. Martinez who leads them in a game of touching their knees, toes and feet. Ms. Martinez calls out the words in English and the children try to keep up.

The words come faster and faster and when Ms. Martinez stops the children fall down. They are giggling.

"Who's tired?" Ms. Martinez asks, catching her breath. No one is tired. No one wants to stop.

6

Full Circle

Miguel Ceballos (University of Texas, MA '90)

O<small>N THE LAST DAY OF HIS FIRST YEAR OF TEACHING</small> at the junior high where years before he had learned to hate school Miguel Ceballos arrived at seven in the morning, an hour before his students. He walked down the long corridor from the office, out into the lunch area, around the first row of trailers, across the basketball courts until he at last arrived at the beige trailer where he had spent the year trying to find a way to reach students who seemed familiar but remained beyond his reach. The room was quiet, as were the streets of East Los Angeles.

A cloud of smog hung over streets where the few tall buildings were locked and shuttered. Only they and the eucalyptus trees broke the monotonous plane of single family houses that, where not abandoned, sagged in disrepair. The streets were empty and still until the cars started coming.

They drove up East Sixth Street toward Hollenback Junior High School in a haphazard caravan of teachers, who parked in a lot surrounded by a high, Cyclone fence, and parents who bade quick goodbyes to children who then lingered in the courtyard in front of the art deco entrance. Young men with no business at the school other than making their presence felt, slowly and menacingly rumbled by in squat station wagons. The street shook with the music from their outsized speakers.

Miguel sat at his desk in the corner of his temporarily tranquil classroom, preparing for a day that was, in many ways, a microcosm of all the school days that preceded it: if his students never wanted to be in school they especially did not want to be there on the last day, when grades were in and, with the burning off of the morning haze, the sun shining. This morning, as on all the previous mornings, Miguel faced the same perplexing question: How do I make them want to be here?

He knew that many would not even bother showing up and that those who did would be itching to get outside. His classroom door opened onto the vast playground, where twenty-five basketball hoops and many friends looked far more inviting than yet another morning of math. He knew he could not force them to stay, or give them busy work because then they would not even bother to say goodbye before walking out. But he was not about to show a movie or dismiss them early. That was not why he had come back. He had come to teach, and also to make his students see school not as the "prison" in which he once felt trapped, but as a place of possibilities.

He'd hoped to teach history but was instead assigned math, a subject he'd liked before he started hating school. Early in the term, as he thought of ways to make fractions and decimals and geometry accessible, he remembered one of the unspoken pleasures of mathematics — unspoken, that is, in school. "Math," he would say, "was seeing things differently. We tend to think math is $1 + 1 = 2$. Math teaches logic and asks questions differently. In real life we run into problems, and solutions are not always obvious. But to learn math you have to look at things differently."

On the first day of class he held out a rope and then, without releasing his hands, tied a knot. The students liked that because it looked like a trick and tricks were seldom part of school. But then he explained to them that by looking at things in differently — the way they watched him tie the knot — they could see the world, and their place in it, in a new way.

But now, at the close of the term, it seemed to Miguel that once the novelty of his rope trick passed and the class returned to the numbing routine of struggling to manipulate numbers, they slid back into seeing school and themselves in the narrow and hopeless way they had carried with them through elementary school and into junior high. Math confirmed what they'd long suspected: that in this world there were many wrong answers and only one right answer and if you did not know the right one you were stupid or lazy or merely unfortunate.

"They sense that this country is not theirs," he said. "That this school is not theirs. That their future is real limited." He had come back to Hollenback wanting to make them see they were wrong. He'd hoped that he might help them see this through math. But now he wondered whether he had made any difference at all.

He asked himself, "What am I doing? How am I failing? I come home feeling it's so hard. What kind of impact am I making?"

He remembered what it was like being one of them. He remembered teachers who took the joy out of learning and who instead harangued him with questions about his plans for the future, a future that seemed very far away when he was thirteen. He remembered, too, how he'd learned to avoid trouble with the gangs who dominated life at school, how to keep from sitting at the wrong table at lunch and how to stay clear of the side streets just after dismissal. He remembered himself as the small, quiet boy who had gone through elementary school as his teachers' pet, but who sat through class after class at Hollenback convinced "that there was nothing they could teach me." He remembered dreaming of dropping out at sixteen and moving to Canada to avoid the draft. "The last thing in the world I wanted to be was a teacher," he said, laughing at the memory. "And here I am."

In the weeks before the end of the term the talk in the teachers' room was of budget cuts and layoffs which for Miguel meant there was no assurance of a job in the fall. All he could be sure of in his newfound career as a teacher was today and today he was not going to surrender to the powerful diversion of the last day of class. He had been fighting diversions all year — from the gangs, apathy, and failure, to pressure to keep pace with the curriculum timetable, to the maddening attitude that said that those who studied were fools. How much tougher could the last day be than all the days that preceded it?

At eight o'clock, after reveille and the Pledge of Allegiance echoed over the loudspeakers, his first class, the seventh graders, burst into the room. Today, he told them, they were going to play baseball. For prizes. In their seats. With numbers. Dodgers versus Angels.

Then he smiled his gentle smile and asked, "Who wants to go first?"

*   *   *

Miguel Ceballos returned to Hollenback Junior High School caught between the intellectual pull of academia and the desire to be a social activist in practice rather than in theory. He had done both, and now, at the age of thirty-six, still found himself searching. Having taught once, he wanted to return to the classroom, to get the kind of "grounding" that graduate studies, no matter how rigorous, could not provide. Yet he feared that if he waited too long to go back to school, if he and his wife Carmen Pacheco started a family, he might never return. It was Carmen who first heard of Teach for America. They were living in Austin, where Miguel was completing his Master's Degree in Latin American Studies at the University of Texas. Teach for America offered them the chance to teach for two years. Then they could decide about the future.

Miguel's ambivalence was not new. He began college at Loyola Marymount, a Catholic school in Los Angeles, but after two years left to work for the United Farm Workers. He helped organize the boycott against California growers and organized workers in the fields and then, after two years, decided to go back to school. Rather than return to Loyola Marymount — a school, he says, that admitted him as part of an affirmative action admissions program despite mediocre high school grades — he wanted to go to Berkeley. Miguel did not think himself ready for Berkeley, and so first spent two years at Cal State-Los Angeles, re-learning the lessons he'd too casually approached at Loyola Marymount. He combined his study with work, first assisting an elementary school math teacher and then working at a halfway house for mentally disordered ex-offenders.

Miguel earned a degree in Chicano Studies at Berkeley, met Carmen, who was then a student at Mills College in Oakland and, upon graduation returned to a life as an activist, this time lobbying on the behalf of University of California students. He spent four years in Sacramento and then, having never traveled further south than the Mexican border towns, left for three months on the first of two trips to Mexico and Central America.

He traveled deep into Mexico, and then on to Honduras, Guatemala and Panama. He met relatives, made friends and saw a dimension of poverty that eclipsed anything he had known growing up in the housing projects of East L.A. Years later he found himself fusing those memories — getting off the bus at night in Guatemala City and seeing men sleeping in the street and smelling their excrement — with childhood memories of walks with his brothers through Los Angeles' skid row and wondering why no one helped the men sleeping in the doorways.

Between the trips Miguel drove a cab in Oakland. He worked as a warehouse stock boy. When the traveling ended he and Carmen returned to Oakland. Miguel wanted to teach.

All that Oakland asked of its substitutes was bachelor's degree. Armed with that and little else, Miguel stepped into the first of many high school classrooms, innocently believing that he was going to teach Spanish and history. Instead the students yelled at him and walked around the room. It was all he could do to keep them quiet. He would ask himself "Why were they behaving this way? I thought the students would be interested in learning because they were in school." Of Oakland, he says, there are no memories of success. After a year he left for Austin and graduate school.

He had grown up the seventh of thirteen children. His father, a Mexican immigrant, was a janitor on the Central Pacific Railroad who worked long hours and, aside from the occasional use of the belt — fighting with siblings was not tolerated — left the rearing of his children to his Chicano wife, Mary. For all that he shared with his friends, and chief among that was poverty, Miguel understood at an early age that his family was different. This was most apparent in the matter of faith, which in the Ceballos home was not Catholicism but Atheism. Mary Ceballos explained to her children that when they were teased about not attending church they were either to ignore the taunts or say that their family was not like everyone else's.

Then there was the matter of school. There were other parents who were strict and others who pushed their children to study. But Miguel believes that what made his family one that produced five college graduates and four teachers — all his siblings attended college, at least for a while — was the simple matter of not merely talking about school, but of teaching. The teaching began with Mary Ceballos, who tutored the older children in letters and numbers. They, in turn, taught the younger ones, "not because they wanted to," Miguel says, "but because my mom said, 'Help them.'" Mary Ceballos taught her children Spanish and, on Saturdays, took them to the neighborhood library. If they wanted to go to the big library downtown they walked, because there was no money for the bus.

Carmen, too, was a seventh child in a large family where for reasons that were not always stated but nonetheless understood, school mattered. While Miguel's family crowded into apartments where, at times, all the children slept in one room (later four or five would share), Carmen's parents were migrant farmers whose children learned that, if nothing else, school could save you from a nomadic life picking fruit and vegetables. Carmen was five years old when she began joining her parents and siblings in the fields. She picked walnuts, cherries and boysenberries. She started at five in the morning and worked till two in the afternoon. Her brothers picked grapes and like them Carmen learned that it was easier to endure cuts and scratches on your hands because the brambles only tore gloves to shreds. Besides, your hands sweated in the gloves and you could not pick as well which meant that you could not pick as much. Picking was a volume business where time was not a measurement of a day's work but something to be battled.

"We were experienced with those options," Carmen would say of the life that awaited the uneducated. The other option, the school option, was personified by her older brother, Lupe. Lupe went to college and then to graduate school, earning a degree in social work. It was not only her parents who expected good things of Carmen in school, but her teachers, too, who knew how well her brothers and sisters had done.

For Miguel elementary school was just as embracing as the time spent learning from his older sisters Olga and Lidia. Years later he would recall how teachers from Miss Triggs in kindergarten to Miss Misneras in sixth grade were kind to him, letting him take the roll and be class monitor even though he was shy and did not seek such privileges. What he enjoyed most was learning because learning helped satisfy his curiosity about the way the world worked. He liked reading and science and math, too, because math was logical and even when it got dull he could still do well on the drills and get a nod and smile from the teacher.

But if elementary school was a "safe place" then Hollenback was nothing of the sort. At Hollenback Miguel was introduced to the idea of school as a place to fear. And there was much to be afraid of, especially from the gangs whose torments the teachers seemed either powerless or uninterested in stopping. "I was afraid of getting hurt," he says. "You didn't want to look at anybody the wrong way. You learned to stay away from crowds, to stay inside at lunch instead of going outside, to go from class to class fast."

There was little time for learning in class because teachers were forever caught up with discipline, which meant that they had little time for shy and studious boys like Miguel who caused them no problems.

"It was hard to get their attention," he says. "In elementary school I bought into the whole notion of the American Dream. I believed what the teachers were telling me. A lot of kids didn't and I was surprised — how can you not believe what the teachers said?

More and more the lessons felt empty. And as he slipped further and further from his teachers' view, the joy Miguel once felt about being in school evaporated. In its place came boredom and with the boredom came disappointment and bitterness. He felt as his students would one day feel: that school had let him down. He could not wait to get out.

*   *   *

Sandra's Dodgers win the coin toss and lead off. Mr. Ceballos explains the rules: fractions in the first inning, decimals in the second and in the third, if there is time, geometry. The easiest questions count as singles, with doubles, triples and home runs coming with increased difficulty. If you answer incorrectly and the other team answers correctly, you're out.

Mr. Ceballos asks Sandra what she wants to try for and Sandra says, "Triple, Mister." The students all call him Mister, even the ones who give him the roughest time.

Mr. Ceballos writes 5/6 divided by 2 1/2. Sandra converts 2 1/2 to 5/2, completes the problem, and waits at third as Darryl comes to bat. Darryl wants to go for a single. Mr. Ceballos writes 2/7 + 5/7 and Darryl quickly writes 7/7.

"You have to reduce if you can," says Mr. Ceballos. The class is quiet as Darryl stares at 7/7. He puts down the chalk. Carla of the Angels comes to the board. She writes 1. Sandra stays at third.

Jason tries for a triple. He mutters "oh shit," when Mr. Ceballos writes 4 divided by 3 1/2.

First Jason writes 7. He erases that. He writes more numbers. He is running out of room on the board as he finishes his calculations with 1 1/7. Sandra scores. Jason is on third, squirming as Susan works out her problem at the board but forgets to reduce 3/9 to 1/3.

Two out. Darryl bites a fingernail. Sandra checks with Jason who tells her "triple."

Mr. Ceballos writes 8 1/9 divided by 2 1/9. Sandra starts multiplying quickly and somehow ends up with 8 1/9. She erases everything and starts again. When she writes the number 4, Darryl says, "that was easy Mister. Even I could do that."

But he goes for another single. And as he subtracts 1/12 from 7/12 Jason holds his hands over his face, waiting for Darryl to reduce. Darryl pauses and holds the chalk to the blackboard, stopping short of 1/2.

"That's three outs," says Mr. Ceballos as Darryl pleads, "But I reduced."

They did well with fractions, not just today but all term long. Decimals was another matter. Decimals eluded them for reasons that Miguel could never quite understand. They remained abstractions, and no matter how hard he tried he could not make them see that decimals differed from fractions only in the way they were written. Like fractions they were symbols. But the symbols made no sense.

"Decimals destroy them," he said. "Either they're not prepared or they hate it. One day you'll teach and the next day they'll forget. I tried doing it by rote learning and that doesn't work. I give them problems and they like it but most can't do them. A quarter will get it and the others will fail."

*   *   *

Several years ago a team of researchers studied the mathematical skills of school-aged Brazilian street vendors. The researchers were struck by the fact that these boys, without any formal math education, were nonetheless able to perform with astonishing speed the calculations necessary in the market. They could add, subtract, multiply and divide large numbers in their heads. But when asked to sit down and calculate numbers they were lost. They were lost because in a school setting the numbers were merely symbols, abstractions. In the market the numbers had a context and the boys had learned to work with them because it was a skill necessary for their work. The numbers, in their lives, were real and dynamic and they had learned to master them as a way of solving the constant problems thrown at them: If apples are five for a thousand *cruzieros*, how much are seven? Fast. They learned because they had to find a way to come up with the right answers, or at the very least answers close enough to avoid being cheated.

The boys were learning math. Real math, not "school" math. In their world it was the "real" math that mattered. School math mattered only one place, and that was in school.

Math and science share the dubious educational distinction of being the subjects that people remember the way they do root canal: necessary but painful. Like science education, math remains a discipline that all but invites failure because, like science, it is too often presented as a series of abstractions at the end of which exists a single correct answer. If success in science is often a matter of, say, correctly defining the word *mitosis,* without necessarily understanding the life of the cell, then math education is often even more remote. At least in science there are familiar looking words. In math there are symbols (numbers) accompanied by another set of symbols (+, -, x, ÷) that dictate the manner in which those numbers are to be manipulated.

The numbers and signs, in the minds of generations of school children, do not exist, as they were intended to exist, to solve problems; they are the problems. School math is about "solving problems," as in "class, open your workbooks and solve the problems on page 43."

"Mathematics is the only place where we make the mistake of trying to teach you the answer first and come back later and try to teach you the question," says Robert Davis, dean of the Rutgers University School of Education, and for many years a leader in the effort to reform math education. "You invent math to understand. Traditionally it has to have been the case that the human race had problems and solved problems. Where did counting come from? It has to have been that people wanted to keep count of things: sheep, or the fish in the Nile. People wanted to know boundaries and had to invent ways to calculate them. Notice that this is the opposite of what happens in school. The whole process is meaningless."

Meaningless because the numbers exist in a vacuum. Even if they are placed in an artificial context — "how many

Big Macs can I buy with $6.73 and how much change will I have?" — school seldom gives children the chance to work with those numbers, play with them, move them around in a effort to find a way to see how they might help solve a problem.

Davis tells the story of a periodic feature on the old television show "Candid Camera." People were asked to divide 1/3 by 1/2. And time and again, he says, they couldn't. They'd say things like, "How can you divide 1/3 by 1/2 if 1/3 is bigger?" The numbers were no more real to them as adults than they'd been when they were children. Yet we continue asking school children to answer just such questions, to solve just such meaningless problems. We don't necessarily ask them to understand, only to be able to divide 1/3 by 1/2. On the test.

I told Davis that while I embraced the premise, I could not see how to move from idea to practice. Davis is one of those wonderful teachers whose enthusiasm grows as he begins explaining things. He started talking about situations — problems — and how you could devise ways for solving them, not by dividing 1/3 by 1/2 but by thinking of other ways to pose the question.

But here was the problem: Davis and I were speaking on the phone, which meant that all I had were representations of what he meant, words and numbers that I could not see, or touch. I asked him to stop and Davis, a man as gentle as he is determined to see math education revolutionized, explained that the bewilderment I was feeling was just what so many students feel because they are removed from the numbers they are asked to use.

Eager to make the abstract real I sought out a protege of Davis' closer to home. His name was Hal Melnick and as a professor of mathematics education at Bank Street College of Education in New York, taught teachers how to teach math. The overwhelming majority of teachers he encountered, Melnick explained, felt themselves to be poor mathematicians and had few good memories of the subject in school. Yet now they were being asked to teach math to students who probably carry from school the same feelings as their teachers.

I wanted to know where the process broke down. My memory of school was of teachers forever offering scenarios, attempting to ground a problem in a situation which was, at the very least, imaginable. I offered one: if I have twenty-one pencils and six friends, how many pencils does each friend get if I'm dividing them equally.

There was nothing wrong with the question, he said. The trouble began with what followed. He explained that the teacher in all likelihood would write the numbers 21 and 6 on the board and then commit what the reformers saw as the cardinal sin of math education. He or she would tell the class the way to answer the question. The way. The one, single, fool-proofed, burnish-this-into-your-minds way of — and here came another bit of jargon — of DIVIDING twenty-one by six in order to find that right answer.

At this point Melnick reached not for the chalk, but for the toys. We sat in a room filled with shapes and books and cut-outs and all manner of things that teachers could carry into the classroom so that not they, but their students, could touch the numbers they were working with. He placed on the desk a box filled with yellow squares and red squares and then another box filled with little bears. He did not say the word divide. He just let me play.

I took six little bears and placed them in a row. These represented my friends. I spread out twenty-one yellow squares: the pencils. One by one, as if I were dealing cards, I gave each friend a pencil. And when I was finished doling them out, each had three. Except that I had three left over. What to do with the other three? I took out six red squares and decided that these represented half pencils. Now, I asked, how did I know that one pencil split in half equal two? Melnick, reminding me that knowledge is cumulative (I may have learned this the day before) said, You know. Each friend then got a red square to go with his three yellow ones.

But I was not done. I still had to explain, precisely, how I did it. I had to explain my "formula" for concluding that each friend got three and a half pencils. But there was no rush; I could take all the time as I needed.

If all this seems laughably obvious I should explain what was happening down the hall. There, in a room decorated with the class' artwork — "our 8s"; renderings of the number in toothpicks and shapes — sat teachers learning to teach math.

They sat in groups of three and four, the better to work together in the manner that reformers say helps students learn not alone but from each other. They too were playing with shapes. But before they even started doing that they clapped their hands and snapped their fingers. The lesson today was on patterns. First the teacher had everyone snap their fingers twice and clap their hands once. The class did this a few times until they had the pattern down. Then she told them to represent the same pattern with their shapes.

One woman made a simple pattern — a line of two yellow diamonds followed by a blue diamond — while a man made his in a circle to represent infinity. Another woman made her's with two hexagons followed by two half hexagons. And, as if to remind everyone else how quickly adults assume the roles they once played as children in the classroom, a woman sitting in her group leaned over and, like the kind of kid who all but begged to get beat up after class, raised her hand and said, "That's not right. That's not the right pattern. She has two half hexagons and that's not the pattern."

The teacher walked over and rather than say what teachers sometimes do — "why don't you mind your own business"

— instead reminded her that there were no absolutes in this exercise. Her classmate could represent the pattern any way she wanted, as long as in the end she could demonstrate that the method that she devised reproduced the pattern that everyone had heard and performed. It was not until the teachers-cum-student did this several times that they took out their number boards and began searching for patterns in the numbers from one to one hundred.

What their teacher was doing was showing them how a teacher could lead a class of students in making their own discoveries. Too often, Melnick explained, because the teacher effectively says that only he or she knows the way of solving the problem students come to believe not only that all knowledge resides in the teacher, but that any alternative is wrong. They are seldom if ever given the chance to conquer the problem themselves, to find strategies that might help them make sense of the world. The result, he says, is both passivity and a growing sense of incompetence.

Yet schools by and large continue measuring progress in math by the very methods that undercut the possibility of change. The standardized, multiple-choice tests that assess success and failure, Melnick said, were an outgrowth of the military's attempt during World War I to educate as quickly as possible illiterate recruits in the skills necessary for military service. Even the early proponents of such tests insisted that they were designed only for retaining knowledge for the short term. And yet they endure as the holy grail of education, the benchmark by which generations of students are measured. Schools teach for the test and measure their own success by the tests. But all the tests prove is how well students scored on them, not what they know.

"Why does it persist?" asked Robert Davis. "You can't get the American people to understand that what test scores do is test abstractions only. We don't want questions. What's holding it in this wrong posture is people are checking the wrong things all the time. By attempting to impose order on it there is no order."

That meant that while schools could introduce any number of new ways of teaching math, teachers knew that at the end of the term their students had to be prepared for standardized tests. And the tests changed everything. So too did the curriculum timetable. Like Jill Gaulding in her science class, Miguel Ceballos wanted to spend more time making sure that his students learned. He would have preferred not having to rush to cover the units mandated in the course guide. But what was he to do? Ignore it and risk having his students score poorly on the tests? Carmen, who taught kindergarten, had spent much of the year introducing her students to reading and writing by getting them to think of words as tools to explain their worlds. And then at the end of the term Carmen learned that her students were going to be tested.

Carmen would come home and tell Miguel, "These kids are saying, 'Why are you making me take this test?'" They would look at her and ask, 'What's the right answer?'" effectively undoing everything she'd spent a year trying to teach them about reading and writing, and also, Carmen and Miguel both felt, undermining whatever trust those students had in their teacher and in school. Why should they trust a teacher, Miguel asked, if all they were going to get for their troubles in the end was a test that confirmed what they did not know?

"Its very hard for a teacher to say that's not what I should be teaching," says Robert Davis. "We set up the task so the teacher almost has to fail."

Hollenback had been selected as part of the Coalition of Essential Schools, the Rhode Island-based program established by Theodore Sizer to help bring reform to the nation's secondary schools. When the CES representative came for a workshop at Hollenback, Miguel listened to his suggestions and ideas for change and then asked how he was supposed to give his students time to make independent discoveries about numbers if he did not have the hours to give them?

"Now you go through the whole curriculum and half your students fail," replied the CES representative. "Maybe a quarter get a C. If you do it this way at least they'll learn something."

But here Miguel doubted his ability. Perhaps if he was more experienced, he reasoned, he would know how to implement these new ideas in a way that let his students keep pace. But then he thought of the limited skills his students carried with them from elementary school to Hollenback and grew even more disheartened.

"I'm trying to make math more relevant to the real world, like doing decimals by having them work on a budget," he said. "I told them, Suppose you're not in school and you have job and you're making six dollars an hour. You're lucky and don't have to pay taxes. What will you buy? They clipped out ads and brought them in. We factored in rent, utilities, food. And your budget had to balance. For a couple of days it was okay. And then we had to move on. They liked it for a while. Some of them messed around. The problem is the guidelines the state issues. It's ridiculous to get them to go through it so quickly. I want to just focus on a few topics and spend more time on them. Make projects relate to other projects."

But even if he could interest them, there was no assurance that they'd want to be challenged. Miguel tried, for instance, to relate measurement to outer space. He reasoned that perhaps they might be interested in learning to measure, to use the skills of reading numbers and working with exponents and decimals, to calculate how far the planets were from one another.

But when he explained the project his students said, "Why are we doing this? This isn't math."

"They would say, 'Why don't we go back to the other way?'" said Miguel. "They were used to that. They're not interested in learning math, per se. They're putting in their time. They don't want to think if they don't have to. Like how to relate math to a real life situation because what they learned all these years is 'do the work, do the minimum and you'll have no trouble.'"

So Miguel, like so many other teachers, was left to count his successes in the most modest way. At least he could get his seventh graders to want to play math baseball on a day when they were itching to get outside. The eighth graders were another matter.

"You're gonna make us work?" they ask as they walk into class.

Like the seventh graders they would play baseball for pencils. And like the seventh graders they play for a while. But now, in the late morning, with their friends coming by the door, beckoning them to come out, and the schoolyard filling up with students who'd already abandoned class, they begin drifting toward the door.

Some leave; a few come back and forth, talking with their friends and then taking their turn in the game. The game began with the boys against the girls. But as the end of the period nears and even those who'd lingered at Mr. Ceballos' desk now grab their books and hurry outside, only one student remains.

His name is Eddie and before he leaves he is going to go for a home run by adding 5 2/4 and 8/7 and then subtracting 2 1/2. Eddie is a quiet student who does his work and caused no problems. Lately he has fallen in with a group of boys who spend their time dancing in hip hop dance contests. Eddie was gaining a reputation as a fine dancer.

But now, even as the bell rings, he presses his face close to the board, struggling with the problem. He looks at the numbers and writes his answer. The period is over and he is free to go but he waits as Mr. Ceballos gently explains why he got it wrong.

Eddie grabs his books. He lingers at the door before calling out "See you later Mister."

And then, like all his classmates, he is gone.

*　　　*　　　*

When Miguel Ceballos talked of why he became a teacher he spoke of a lesson learned from Cesar Chavez, the late founder of the United Farm Workers union. Miguel, then a young organizer, was struck by Chavez' simple message of being willing to help other people by sacrificing something of yourself.

Now, years later, he clings to that message, yet cannot shake the memory of what happened to the teachers he had had who, like him, wanted to "make a change." "I seemed to remember," he said, "that people who were really committed don't last very much.

"I keep asking, 'What am I doing wrong here?' I'm seeing students who I began with, going from being interested in school, who are now failing. They're in gangs. You can see the change in their faces. You try all of this and its not working. And the kids will tell you. There are some kids who enjoy school and then they'll tell you how much they hate you. Kids who used to like me and who now tell me that they hate me. I'm losing them and they're my kids. But I realize I have them for an hour a day. I can't win them over by myself. I guess I shouldn't worry about it. I'm not a psychologist. I'm a teacher but after you have them for a while you bond with them, you care about them."

Jose Gomez was one of those students. Jose was big and in a school like Hollenback this was a curse because people expected him to act like a man. Jose got into fights and joined a gang and once spent a month on detention. He was one of the students who disrupted every class he sat in. And yet Miguel saw in him not an nuisance but a big lost boy.

"He needs someone he feels he can trust," he would say. And then, almost apologetically, he would add, "He trusts me." Jose trusted Miguel because Miguel understood when it was necessary to protect Jose. The protection he needed was from his father, whose response to calls from school and poor grades was a beating and an accusation that Jose was nothing but a bum and a fool. Miguel understood that he could use this fear constructively, and so told Jose, "straighten up or I'll call your father."

Jose straightened up, at least for a while. He struggled in all his classes, math included, although he did show some affinity with fractions. Decimals left him lost. Which was why it was so important, and so much cause for celebration, the day that Miguel handed back quizzes on decimals, except for Jose's which he marked with an A and hung in the front of the room. Miguel made him Student of the Week.

But Miguel soon saw that trust was no match for the impediments that a student like Jose Gomez encountered at Hollenback, impediments that could turn a momentarily engaged and trusting student into one who would finish ninth grade without a single passing grade.

Miguel recognized he could not compete with poverty, hopelessness and a sense that school offered nothing because even when you got out you were going to remain an outsider who foolishly wasted his time in the classroom. He saw, too, that while he and Carmen found in school the warmth and acceptance that comes with success, his students found it with the gangs. He could not compete with the gangs, not when he was a student and tried so hard to avoid them, and not as a teacher, when he hoped that by making his students see life in a different way, they might not see the gangs as the only right answer in their lives.

They were never the answer for him. Though five of his nine brothers were in gangs Miguel avoided them. "I was kind of afraid of it," he says. "To get involved you had to fight and get beat up and I wasn't interested in that." Nor did he want to risk incurring the wrath of his father, who turned on his wayward sons with his belt. "I didn't want that either."

Mary Ceballos tried shielding her sons from the gangs. She ordered them to play in the front of the housing project where they lived, rather than out back, near the playground, where the gangs hung out. But her warnings, and her husband's threats, did little good. Miguel still recalls the morning he watched his older brother racing from a policeman who tackled and arrested him in front of the family's house. His mother begged the police not to take her son away and to this day Miguel does not know why his brother was arrested because within the family it became a matter that was not discussed.

Fifty gangs operate in the Hollenback area. There are Mexican gangs, Salvadoran gangs, Colombian gangs. There are new gangs and gangs so old that new members are sometimes the grandsons of charter members. What the older gang members did in dividing their barrios into turf, and warring over it, the younger gang members do with their schoolyards. This begins in grade school. By the time a young man arrives in Hollenback he is already familiar with the gangs, but only on a local level. Now there are new gangs from other elementary schools fighting for the turf of the Hollenback schoolyard, which means that there are lessons to be learned that are far more essential than those the teacher taught.

"He has to know who's fighting who, who to make friends with in class," says Steve Valdivia, director of Youth Gang Services in Los Angeles. "He has to make known who he's aligned with. This is before learning takes place. At lunchtime he has to know who follows him out of class. The bottom line is there are dangers around every corner."

If he did not join a gang then he made it his business to make friends with people who were in gangs, or, at the very least, to wear the baggy pants and shirts or Los Angeles Raiders jackets that the gang members wore. He learned to strut like a gang member. He learned to talk like the gang members talked. Maybe he even gave himself a graffiti nickname, so that people would think he was in a gang. Where once the gang members were the outsiders, now it was those who did not join who stood apart.

It was not always necessary to break the law to be part of a gang. In truth, Valdivia said, maybe only five or ten percent of the gang members were criminals, a percentage that had not changed in many years. The others spent half their time getting high — smoking pot or crack, sniffing glue or paint thinner.

To be in a gang was to thumb your nose at authority, to see yourself as an outcast by joining a society of outcasts. In the gang you could find a place in the world, because more and more the sense of the young men of East Los Angeles and places like it, was that the rest of the world had no use for them.

Miguel, too, remembered leaving his East Los Angeles neighborhood of Boyle Heights for Loyola Marymount and recognizing "that when I was growing up I never had a concept of what it was like outside of Boyle Heights." Though he lived in the dorms he avoided the white students, not only because their music and ideas of fun felt alien, but because he sensed that when they heard the colloquial English he had grown up speaking "they might think that I was dumb."

Now he saw how his students used their fears of failing in that world as an excuse for avoiding the education that could lead them out of East Los Angeles. "They justify not having to go out into the world, saying that they don't really care about getting a certain kind of job," he says. "I think they say it to justify not doing well in school. I don't know if they think it's too scary to try."

So, violent as they were, the gangs still felt safer than the world beyond because at least in a gang you knew that if you were loyal to your brothers they would be loyal to you.

"Gangs are not the beginning," Valdivia said. "They are the end. Gangs are not the introduction to life. They are the end of the road. When young people have decided that education sucks, when they've taken away the parks and after school activities, when parents and society are lying to them, when they may not know the meaning of the word dysfunctional but they know what it means, then you join a gang and that is the ultimate in despair. They are the result. They are not the cause. And gang members, the violent ones, act out the anger and despair of a community."

I told him about Miguel, about his background and about the way he cared for his students and wanted so badly to make a difference in their lives. Perhaps, Valdivia said, he could, "if he's a cool teacher. If there were more of him, back then, twenty-five years ago, what a difference that would have made. That's the loudest message you can give the kids: who is in charge of you."

For years, he explained, the message was that the people in charge were from someplace else — the San Fernando Valley, Ventura County — and that at the end of the day that was where they returned. The message was that the degree of caring from these people was limited, if it existed at all. And so what the kids learned was that the only caring they could count on was from one another, from their cohorts in their gangs.

"If you could turn the clock back twenty-five years and if more of him were there we would not be talking about this," Valdivia said. But now, he added, "He's a light bulb in a sea of darkness and the amount of light is limited as far as it travels. If he follows a historical pattern, he'll get burnt out and move on. There's too much that he has to deal with that's wrong. He's fighting the same battle the kids are. And the kids are let down again. And I do stress again."

Miguel, too wondered how long he might go on, how long before he began to see that too little came from too much trouble. "Maybe in three, four or five years I'll be a better teacher," he said. "But after six or seven years I'll find out that no matter how good a teacher I am I won't be as successful as I want to be."

*   *   *

And then something would happen that reminded him that perhaps Carmen was right when she told him, after yet another lament about how much the students hated him, that he was getting through in ways he could not always see.

It happened in unexpected ways, like the night he chaperoned a dance at school. He brought Carmen and introduced her to his students. And just by doing that, he says, "maybe they felt that they were important enough to introduce them to a part of my life." In the weeks that followed the dance he saw the difference that simple introduction made to students like Diana, who had done little but sneer at him but who grew closer to him. "She felt," Miguel says, "that I was willing to trust her."

Such moments were elusive, but when they came they reminded Miguel that maybe he was indeed "making a change" in his work.

So it was on the last day of class that Mr. Ceballos addressed the seventh graders. "It was a very enjoyable class," he said. "It was my best class."

Sandra asked, "Are we the best class you ever had?" and he replied, "I was teaching once before, in Oakland, and this class is better. You guys are very motivated and try real hard. I saw some of the best in Hollenback in my classes. Keep it up and you'll do well in eighth grade."

Then Carla asked, "Are you gonna be here next year?"

"I hope, unless they lay me off," he replied

Veronica asked, "This will be hard for teachers."

"Yes, some will have salaries cut."

He joked about wanting to be in an air conditioned classroom next year and then told them, "I said yesterday I'd give prizes to those who won the game."

With that Mr. Ceballos began handing out pencils for the winners. The pencils had Mickey Mouse and Garfield the Cat on them. And at that moment you could see that even though these seemed like the last prize that children hardened by poverty and gangs would want, they crowded around his desk, reaching for them. Jason, whose team lost, tried grabbing for one and Mr. Ceballos reminded him with a smile that they were for the winners.

Before the game, Mr. Ceballos had asked them to sign his year book — "but no bad words."

Now, in the quiet before the eighth graders arrived, he read what the students wrote to him.

"To Mr. Ceballos, the coolest, freshest, teacher I ever had."

"Mister You are cool and are very nice. Hey Mister have a quiet summer and be happy."

"Hope to see you around the school next year.".

"Thank you for caring if I study or not. Mister get ready to give out more homework."

"The only teacher I ever actually learned some math from."

"Call me someday and see what's up. Maybe I'll have a kid. Ha ha."

7

At The End Of The Day

Julie Burstein (University of Michigan, '90)

Julie Burstein's memories of elementary school are of bringing her dog to show and tell, playing kick ball during recess, and of children learning together. School was fun and because Julie carried that memory through high school and the University of Michigan and into her first classroom, she wanted her students to see school as she had.

They did not. When Julie went to school children did not bring bullet cartridges to class and tell stories about cousins who'd been shot. There were no children like Armando who could barely read and write and cried frequently and who one day disappeared, leaving Julie in a panic until the custodian found him just before dismissal. "We sat down and talked," Julie said, "and he listened and made faces and gave me the finger." Nor were there children like Anna who had no father and touched the boys a lot and who hovered around Julie, begging to be hugged. One day Anna handed out to her classmates the ten and twenty dollar bills she'd pilfered from her mother's purse so that the children could buy candy and popcorn, and, hopefully, like her. "She was, in her mind," said Julie, "successful."

Julie attended Martin Luther King, Jr. Elementary School in the Chicago suburb of Evanston, Illinois, where children did not come to school on 100 degree days wearing long-sleeve shirts to hide bruises, and with excuses for parents suspected of abuse. They did not wear clothes that did not fit, or that had not been washed. Nor did they come dressed in their best clothes like America did on her father's birthday because after school she was going to visit him in prison. Julie did not recall mothers like Armando's who came to see her and started crying because she bought her son candy and toys and this did not stop him from misbehaving. Julie listened as Armando's mother pleaded for advice and wanted to say, "You're asking *me?*"

Even on class picture day and assembly days, Julie could not recall coming to school in a party dress and party shoes the way the girls in her class at Stanford Elementary School in Southgate, a Los Angeles neighborhood adjoining Watts, came dressed for the class trip. The boys wore nice pants and bow ties for the trip to Westwood, to the green and tranquil UCLA campus where they saw a Christmas play. The children, Julie learned, had almost never been out of their Los Angeles, a city of abandoned houses and liquor stores with iron bars over the windows, the Los Angeles of the Crips and Bloods and scores of Latino gangs, the Los Angeles that never went to the beach. Now they peered out the window and called to her, because they wanted to tell her what they were seeing. She remembered that day and remembered too the incredulous looks on the children's faces when they asked her, "What do you speak at home?" and she told them "English" and that, no, she did not live at school.

For Christmas her children brought her gifts like a teddy bear and a porcelain swan and asked her to open the boxes right away because they wanted everyone to see what they brought. One brought her mother's skirt.

"A lot of them called me mom," Julie said, "and asked if they could come home with me."

Julie's mom and dad at first were not pleased about her teaching so far away in Los Angeles. Still, when they visited, Julie's mom brought Spanish-language books for her daughter's class. Julie came to Teach for America "a graduating senior without a job," thinking that she might teach for a while before returning to graduate school. She thought that she would study literature, although her fluency in Spanish might help in determining a career.

She started studying Spanish in eighth grade and discovered an immediate affinity for the language. That summer her teacher took her and seven classmates for a trip to Mexico, where they lived in the teacher's big house. Later she went to a Spanish-language camp at Concordia College and then, for a summer, to the Spanish city of Toledo. In school she refined her Spanish through the works of such authors as Cervantes and Garcia Lorca. After graduation she spent another summer in Mexico, this time in Cuenbaca, a city two hours from Mexico City. "My parents," she said, "had money to pay for all these wonderful experiences I had."

Her students were almost all the children of immigrants, or were immigrants themselves. They came from Mexico and Central America and often that is where their parents took them during vacations. Sometimes the children did not come back to school. Sometimes, before they left in the middle of the term, they came to tell her that this would be their last day. Sometimes, they just disappeared. Other children would arrive to take their places.

Like the others they became her responsibility. Despite her desire to make them see school as a welcoming place where they could learn to enjoy learning, Julie soon discovered that this was not always possible, for reasons big and small. The big reasons revolved around poverty and poverty's impact upon families. And while those reasons were most apparent, Julie soon discovered what millions of teachers had discovered before her: that what so often got in the way of teaching was the accumulation of petty obstacles and humiliations that had nothing at all to do with children learning.

*   *   *

It began each morning with her mailbox which, depending on the day of the week or time of the year was crammed with, among many other things, instructions on assemblies, flyers on staff meetings, revised schedules to accommodate parent-teacher conferences, behavior referrals, tardiness notices, instructions on new ways to fill out attendance reports, and announcements that students were supposed to carry home. If the students forgot to bring these announcements to their parents, or forgot to bring back the part of the form their parents were supposed to fill in, Julie would find in her mailbox a reminder that so-and-so's parents had not returned say, a free lunch eligibility form which meant that that child was not eligible for a free lunch. "There was never a day," Julie said, "when there was nothing in my box."

Sometimes Julie would take the papers in her mailbox and stuff them in the drawer of her classroom desk, and sometime later find printed suggestions about celebrating holidays in the classroom. There was considerable risk in not attending to this paperwork immediately because if the announcement required a written response to be sent "downtown" Julie would hear from the people in the office about her delinquency. So each morning Julie began her day attending to any number of bureaucratic responsibilities that eclipsed the mere taking of the roll. Even with the advent of computers, millions of teachers still had to fill out surveys of their class' ethnic breakdown, plow through assembly and line-up instructions, assign lunch numbers — and hope that their children remembered their numbers as they walked through the lunch line — all the while making sure that the form overlooked was not the form that demanded immediate attention. This could take hours.

"And then," Julie said, "you had to have the energy to teach."

Not that she could teach without interruptions because there were always visitors to interrupt her lesson with a knock on the door. There were: Children from the upper grades making an announcement about the book fair; another teacher with a discipline problem in tow, wanting Julie to let the problem child sit in a corner before returning to class: a request for classroom "timeout" that Julie could not refuse because she would make the same one herself; the principal coming to observe; another teacher coming to observe; a group of fifth graders who'd helped her move boxes the day before dropping by to see if she needed a hand with anything; older siblings bringing pens or a lunch ticket or money; the reading specialist; the social worker. Julie said, "There was always somebody at the door."

Sometimes parents came by to watch. Most of the time they just wanted to see their child in class and sometimes they asked questions in the middle of a lesson. One mother came to class from time to time and asked vague questions about homework or a lunch ticket that left Julie unsure of what she wanted: "She didn't seem to know either." Julie was always struck, five minutes into a phone call from offices of friends who were not teachers, that they were talking on the phone at work. She could talk on the phone, during her lunch break, but that was not always possible because she had lunch with her class and often accompanied them to recess. She could use the bathroom, too, during her prep period.

Then there were extras. Julie knew it would be a good day when at eight o'clock the lady from the office did not appear at the door with six more second graders and say, "take them."

Julie had learned in the teachers' lounge that the children who appeared at the door as the bell was ringing were called "extras," — as in "who has extras?" — and had learned from experience that "extras" could ruin your day, especially if you got, say, four or five. If you got six extras on top of your classroom limit of thirty you were supposed to get more money in your next paycheck. But only if you had six. Except that she had had six and never gotten a penny.

The arrival of extras, in whatever number, meant that whatever lesson she had planned for the day was immediately rendered obsolete: she had planned for a group of thirty and thirty-six children meant a different class entirely. The extras had not necessarily learned the lesson she had taught the day before and, even if they had, were not accustomed to the way she taught and the way the class worked. The extras needed chairs and desks and paper. They needed pencils and erasers and workbooks and they also needed attention because sometimes the extras would fight with each other and sometimes they'd fight with Julie's children, who did not like getting squeezed even tighter and having to compete with the extras to be noticed. "The children want to know, 'Why are they here?'" Julie said. "One more upheaval in their lives they don't need."

On days when she had extras Julie could forget about individual instruction. She improvised. The class sang songs and did art and listened as she read stories. They worked as a single group. Sometimes they played Simon Sez.

Julie knew that when the lady from the office appeared at her door with extras she could not refuse, just as she'd been unable to refuse the first day of class when the principal told her that even though she'd been hired to teach a bilingual class of second graders she was now going to have a few first graders, too. "You'll do a wonderful job," said the principal, who would then periodically dispatch another first grader for whom Julie had to make room.

Difficult as it was teaching first and second graders together, Julie could still plan for them. That was a luxury that did not exist with extras, a phenomenon endemic to schools like Stanford which, because of their suspect location and student body, could not always attract per diem substitutes when a teacher called in sick. If the principal could not get the art teacher or the gym teacher or the cluster teacher to take the place of their absent colleague, the children were simply split up and sprinkled around the other classes, like so many orphans dispatched to foster homes.

There were never "extras" at King Elementary School, where Julie went. There were substitutes. There were books and sufficient desks and chairs arranged in clusters. There were first and second graders together, but this was by design. King was an experimental public school, where children, a mix of white and black, were encouraged to proceed not according to the proscribed grade level but at their own pace. At King there were twenty children in a class and an ongoing effort to avoid tracking children by their ability. Still, the students knew who was doing well and who struggled, if only because the quicker ones helped the others with their reading and math.

Sometimes, at Stanford, the absent teacher accidentally took the class lunch tickets home. The children arrived in Julie's room without proof that they were eligible for a free lunch or that their parents had paid for their meals. Then there was the matter of their parents looking for their children at the end of the day and not being able to find them because they did not know where they'd been sent and who had been babysitting them.

Today, however, was a good day. "Today," Julie said, "I felt like I helped everyone."

This afternoon, unencumbered by extras, the children worked in their familiar groups. Some made log cabin collages — Lincoln's birthday was approaching — from popsicle sticks and cut out shapes that they pasted onto black construction paper. Others pulled from a box food advertisements clipped from supermarket inserts and flyers. They pasted the ads on paper and then wrote sentences in Spanish about the food in the ads. Two girls jockeyed for position in front of the computer, where they played a math game that asked them to find the number missing from a sequence.

"*Aqui,*" one of the girls said to the other when she could not find the right key to hit.

Julie Burstein walked among them, admonishing the girl hogging the computer to share, admiring another student's work on a crossword puzzle emblazoned on Lincoln's profile, asking still another what Lincoln was doing in the log cabin he'd made. "Reading a book?" she asked.

The girls at the computer, their turn done, asked, "Teacher can we do it tomorrow?" Tomorrow they could because the class still had a few weeks to use the computer before their turn ended and the computer was rolled down the hall to another class, never to be seen again.

At 2:45, after the bell rang and her students raced out the door, into the schoolyard and on toward home, Julie said "This was a good afternoon. No fights. No interruptions."

It was one of those days when school for Julie's children was almost like school as it was for Julie, when she was their age. But this was a rare day, a day when the gulf between Julie's world and that of her students did not feel quite so wide.

It was a day made rarer, too, by the rain that cascaded down and flooded the schoolyard. On their way home the children walked along streets covered with fallen leaves and tree limbs. Julie switched on the windshield wipers as she drove along the streets where the children lived.

Then she left their streets behind and she sped toward the freeway and home.

*   *   *

Julie spent her first year of teaching, not very happily, at an elementary in the nearby neighborhood of Lynwood where such basic supplies as textbooks were at such a premium that she did not have math texts until Thanksgiving. She taught in a poorly ventilated room that on hot days felt like an oven. The teaching assistant she was promised arrived two months into the term and, because her presence was needed for secretarial work, was often called away in the middle of a lesson. Julie had student taught at Stanford, liked the school, and so in the course of her first year wrote to the principal asking whether she might have a place for her in the coming year. The principal wrote back that she'd be pleased to have her.

But Los Angeles was then going through a budget crisis in which teacher hiring was frozen and salaries cut. So in May, Julie went to the district office seeking an official appointment to her new school. She waited on line for two days with perhaps another 150 teachers. Many had been laid off. They came with their children and moved from line to line, hoping to find something. Sometimes they found chairs and sometimes they stood, and no one left the line because that meant risking losing their place. Everyone waited, listened to hear their name called, or to hear whether a position for which they might qualify had opened up.

On the second day Julie heard that bi-lingual teachers were being hired. She hurried to the room, showed the letter from the principal, a certificate attesting to her bi-lingual proficiency and signed a contract. She was lucky. She found a job. She was not subjected to the demeaning process that even veteran teachers describe, of being sent to a school with a group of other teachers who are known collectively as "bodies." The "bodies" wait at the counter in the main office until the principal sees them and tells them what they will be teaching the following Monday. My mother, who'd left the New York City public schools for several years to be an assistant principal in a private school, lost her seniority when she returned to the public schools and with it her job during the city's severe financial crisis in 1974. She tells of waiting in a hiring hall and at last being dispatched to a distant school, arriving at the desk, and hearing the principal on the phone asking not very quietly of the district office, "did you have to send me such old ones?" She was then forty-nine.

*   *   *

Julie Burstein was twenty-three years old and for all that separated her world from that of her students, they were nonetheless connected by language. That she could speak both the language they spoke at home and the nation's language of power and wealth, meant that like so many other bilingual teachers, Julie was a crucial bridge.

There has been bilingual education, and questions about it, in American schools since the eighteenth century. Where once the controversy focussed on German immigrants opening their own schools and teaching their children in their own language, the debate in the past three decades has centered not around one language, but scores. Bilingual education is not just about Spanish, although in Los Angeles, for instance, 800,000 of the one million students in bilingual classes are Spanish speakers. But bilingual education is also about such other languages as Mandarin, Cantonese, Hmong, Korean, Japanese, Laotian, Vietnamese, Russian, Urdu, Hindi, Tagalog and Bengali. It is, on one hand, about all these languages and, on the other, about one language, English, and what it represents in this country. There have been repeated attempts in the course of the nation's history to declare English America's official language. The idea has won approval on the state level, but not nationally.

Even if English is not an official language it remains the language of commerce, politics, and influence. Recognizing that, generations of immigrants have come to this country and then taken the often painful step of learning English. What they spoke at home was another matter entirely. The idea was to learn English for work, for the bus, and for the phone, because otherwise America would be limited to countrymen who understood you.

But it is easy, in the convenient telescoping of immigration history, to think that immigrants all learned to speak English, and all made sure that their children learned the language, too. That, however, was not always the case. What made the lives of the turn-of-the-century immigrants different from those who now comprise the nation's second greatest wave of immigration, was jobs. If you came here in, say, 1915 and never learned to speak much, if any, English you could nonetheless find any number of respectable, if physically taxing jobs. No longer. The past twenty-five years have witnessed a steep decline in the kinds of blue-collar jobs in which immigrants found not only work but a respectable place in America. In their place have come jobs that, even at the bottom level, often require language. You cannot work at Burger King if you cannot take an order.

Neither proponents nor opponents of bilingual education dispute the idea of retaining a native language, and of using that language as a means of sustaining a culture in a new country. Where they differ is in how best to prepare the children of the newly arrived to be able to function first in school and then in the workplace in English.

Since 1968 the federal government has required schools to provide some kind of language assistance to non-English speaking students. How they choose to do this is up to them. The idea was to close the gap between immigrant and native children, one that had left the former with disproptionately higher rates of dropping out and failure. Such failure did not begin with the influx of Asian and Spanish speaking immigrants. In his book *Bilingual Education: History, Politics, Theory and Practice,* James Crawford writes that only 13 percent of the immigrant children in New York City public schools who were twelve years old in 1908 went on to college, as opposed to 32 percent of the children who were white and native-born. In the 1960s the drop-out rate for Puerto Ricans in New York was 60 percent; in 1963 only 331 Puerto Ricans received academic diplomas from New York's high schools and only twenty-eight went on to college.

The years that followed the law's enactment saw any number of programs designed to work immigrant children into the linguistic mainstream, from "sink or swim" approaches in which they had no choice but to learn to speak English, to remedial programs, to dividing the curriculum between English and foreign-language components. One of the problems, however, was that despite so many educators' best intentions bilingual education came to be seen as the path for failures.

By the time Julie Burstein became a teacher the consensus of opinion favored what was known as the transitional approach, or rather approaches, in which teachers combined English-language instruction with native-language lessons in such subjects as math, science and history. The idea was to keep non-English speaking students learning at the same pace as English speakers, all the while introducing more English into their classes. Depending on the program students would be ready for mainstream classes after third, and in some cases, sixth grade.

In 1991 the Department of Education, in a study citing the success of transitional classes, reported that students in such classes did, indeed, keep up with their English-speaking peers. But the difficulty came in moving them out of bilingual classes. Too often, the report stated, teachers held students in the classes designed to give them the quickest path to the mainstream. The fear was that they were simply not ready to be in class with everyone else.

What has evolved is a system in which the expectations of students in bilingual classes are set low, says Eugene Garcia, a professor at the University of California at Santa Cruz, an expert on bilingual education. For years, he explains, the students in bilingual classes suffered from the *pobrecito* or "this poor child" syndrome. "As long as they had clean hands and a clean face we forget that this is really school and in school we have high expectations," Garcia says. "There are thousands of Latino high school graduates, but unfortunately very few of them go on to college. We're just lucky to get them through school."

Part of the problem, he explains, is that for too long language training stood alone as the means of bringing non-English speaking children into the mainstream. Culture, history and the world that the child came from were seldom considered. "The solution that was packaged was that all we need to do is teach the kids English. But that does not deal with who these kids are," Garcia says. "The programs that really make a difference for those kids don't immediately try to make them like the other kids. It takes a long time and understanding the attributes of those children themselves. And only when you take those into account — poverty, language, color — does it eventually make the difference."

All that and removing the stigma of being a student in a bilingual class. If the idea behind bilingual education is to place those students in classes with English speakers, and ideally make them, at least in the eyes of school, like everyone else, then much the same goal can be achieved, on an interim basis, by bringing English-speakers into bilingual classes. Garcia tells of bilingual classes in places like San Diego where affluent white parents ask to have their children placed in classes where they can be immersed in Spanish, the better to gain fluency in a second language. The result is that the linguistic divide is erased, as two groups of children are forced to communicate with one another in two languages, not just one.

But critics argue that the bilingual education hinders far more than it helps. "It works against the idea of integration," says Rosalie Pedalino Porter, author of *Forked Tongue: The Politics of Bilingual Education*, which criticizes bilingual schooling. "It doesn't give children an equal education. I have a problem with the premise that children will not learn the subject matter if they're not taught in their native language and that they will learn English better if it's delayed for a few years."

Porter, a former bilingual teacher and administrator, argues that rather than help immigrant children achieve parity, bilingual programs keep them apart. "What I discovered was that in giving so much instruction in their native language and so little in English they were essentially separated from the school community longer than they needed to be," she says. "What they needed was a big dose of help in English. I think it's important to have people who can communicate with their parents. But I'm afraid that without the language of power in our society these children are not going to have the opportunities they should have."

Instead, she argues, they should be immersed in English. Rather than go through the experience that she endured when she arrived with her parents from Italy in the 1930s and was placed in an English-speaking class without any preparation or assistance ("eventually I caught on") Porter advocates as speedy a path as possible out of educational dependency on a student's native language, a dependency, she says, that exacts an emotional toll on those children. "I've observed these children and they felt they were treated differently. What I saw with the students was that they felt different."

Porter goes on to take issue with the political underpinnings of bilingual education, insisting that the 1968 law was an outgrowth of the civil rights movement that saw a growing celebration of ethnicity and being different. There is nothing wrong, she says, with keeping a second language; she cites the example of Asian parents who send their children to Korean, Chinese or Japanese school on Saturdays. Rather what disturbs Porter is the idea that, in trying to make things easier, especially for the millions of Spanish-speaking immigrant children in the nation's schools, those students are regarded as somehow less capable than their counterparts.

"If I had my way," she says, "I'd have a truly transitional program that can use Spanish but which makes a concerted effort to reduce the use of the language in the first year."

In the end the debate over bilingual education is not limited to the question of language acquisition. It is how best to help children get out, about their leaving school equipped with the skills that might make the difference between a life on the periphery of the American Dream and a life in the America where Julie Burstein lived, and to which she returned at the end of the day.

*   *   *

Julie and her students were on a semester break the day that a jury in Simi Valley, California, acquitted four white Los Angeles police officers in the beating of a black man, Rodney King.

There were people in the streets as Julie drove home from Los Angeles Airport where she'd dropped off a friend. That night she went to Hollywood for dinner and she saw how the streets were getting ever more crowded.

Soon the looting began. At home Julie and her roommate turned on the television and for the next two days they did little more than sit and watch and eat the leftovers that sat in the refrigerator because it was no longer safe to go outside. They went up the roof where, together with their neighbors, they watched the burning of the chicken restaurant across the street and the looting of the computer warehouse nearby. People carried out hundreds of computers and loaded them into pickup trucks and BMWs and then set the warehouse on fire.

The police drove by and Julie quickly understood that things were worse elsewhere. There were fires every place she looked. In her apartment she could hear the helicopters circling above.

She could not get a flight out of Los Angeles Airport. Finally, she and her roommate booked seats on a dawn flight out of Burbank. Julie packed all her valuables in four suitcases, not knowing whether her building would be torched, too. She began calling taxi companies but no one would drive to the airport. Desperate, she found a man with his own van who was willing to risk the trip.

They left during the curfew. The driver covered the windows with towels because he did not want anyone seeing them. Julie peeked out the window as they drove. The streets were empty and she saw the embers of fires still glowing. At the intersection of Hollywood Boulevard the driver told them to duck down because people were on the street.

They reached the airport at five in the morning. It was like an airport in a city under siege, with people trying to get on flights already overbooked. Julie boarded at sunrise. And as the plane took off she looked down at the city and saw nothing but smoke.

For days afterward she sat in her parents' house "in a trance." Her parents did not want her going back and Julie was torn. She wanted to return and then thought of driving by herself through Watts at six in the morning on her way to school. She worried what might happen if the rioting began again and she was caught in the middle, in a classroom filled with frightened first and second graders. She called friends in Los Angeles who told her that while the rioting was over the tension was not. There were two months to go in the term when Julie called her principal and told her that she would not be returning.

The principal told Julie that she understood her fear and assured her that the rioting had not reached the school. She explained that in addition to finding another teacher to take the class through the end of the term and complete their report cards, she would have to explain to her students that Ms. Burstein would not be coming back to them.

In the weeks that followed Julie thought about her students, about whether one teacher or a succession of teachers had taken her class. "I wonder what they're reading in class and which of the first and second graders grasped the skills," she said. "I wonder what their reflections were after the riots. They'd been off for two months and I was hoping that some of them were still in Mexico and El Salvador when the riots broke out. I wonder whether any of them returned."

She thought of Eliseo who struggled in first grade and whose parents often came to class and rushed to praise him so that he would see how important school was to them. She thought of David, a bright child whose mother was in school, too, and of America, who had come in her pretty dress to visit her father in prison and whose mother came to class and asked how she might help her child in school. She thought of Anna, who'd given away her mother's money so that the other children would like her. She remembered how Anna always needed to be hugged.

These were the memories that Julie Burstein carried back to her America. They are like Ho Chang's memories of Barry who was filled with questions and Liliane who honored him by turning to Ho when she was upset. They are like Jill Gaulding's memories of the three weeks at the end of the term when her students couldn't wait to check on their experiments; like Miguel Ceballos' memory of Eddie at the blackboard trying to hit a math home run after the bell rang on the last day of class; like Vicki McGhee's memories of all the words Deirdre used in her letters and Kimberly used in her questions.

They are like Jane Martinez' memories of the children falling to the floor, laughing and never wanting the games to stop, and like Tom Super's memories of the last day of class in his new school when the children did not want to leave him.

For Julie and the others the memories were rewards and also reminders that there was a reason for all the confusion and frustration and sense of failure they endured for two years, and that was the idea embodied by the image of a hand raised and a child saying, "I know."

In the end, Julie Burstein was going to leave, whether or not she finished the term. In the end, in one way or another, many leave. They move on to other jobs and other lives. And what remains alongside the memories both happy and painful, is a question: Did they make a difference? Was their impact as fleeting as a footprint in the sand? Or did something they say, or something they did light a spark that might make a child see school as they had seen it?

Like Julie Burstein did on the day she went home, they looked down from high above, peering through the smoke below, searching for light.

Epilogue

IN THE SUMMER OF 1992, when their two-year commitment to Teach for America ended, Jill Gaulding was preparing to enter Cornell Law School and Ho Choong Chang, Johns Hopkins Medical School. Ho was spending the summer in Brooklyn at the Jackie Robinson Center at Satellite East Junior High School, teaching science and taekwando. Vicki McGhee, who had majored in Middle Eastern Studies, was taking the courses she would need to begin medical school at UCLA. She planned to apply for a program that brings doctors into inner-city neighborhoods.

Miguel Ceballos and his wife Carmen Pacheco were planning to return for another year of teaching, as were Tom Super and his wife, Tania Gutierrez. Jane Martinez left the classroom to become Teach for America's New York recruiter, but was contemplating a career in journalism. Julie Burstein, foregoing graduate school for the time being, was looking for a job.

Of the 489 original corps members who entered classrooms in the fall of 1990, 342, or 70 percent, fulfilled their two-year commitment. Two hundred and six, or 42 percent were still teaching, most of them in the same schools. Eleven were going to graduate school in education and eighteen were working for Teach for America. While the attrition rate is higher than the 12 percent of all teachers who leave the profession after two years, Teach for America points out that it is still lower than the rate in the schools where the corps members teach.

Teach for America has made good on its promise to bring bright people into troubled schools for two years. It has demonstrated, as the Teacher Corps had years before, the power generated by an individual's belief in his or her capacity to change lives. If this is arrogance, then it is arrogance of the best kind, the sort necessary to withstand the assaults that come from students, parents, administrators, indifferent colleagues, and a system that continues treating teachers as "bodies."

This much is clear: Had Wendy Kopp not created Teach for America, there is little assurance that Jill Gaulding would have found her way to a classroom in Bedford-Stuyvesant and shown a class of students over the last three weeks of the term how exciting their own germination-bag experiments could be. Nor was there any assurance that Ho Chang and Vicki McGhee would have been in the classrooms to prod and comfort. Without Teach for America it is doubtful whether Miguel Ceballos would have returned to Hollenback Junior High or Jane Martinez to Washington Heights or whether for all his trouble in Brooklyn, Tom Super would have been in Los Angeles on the last day of school, being the kind of teacher whom his young students did not want to leave. It is doubtful, too, whether Julie Burstein, despite her painful and premature departure, would have been at Stanford Elementary School, helping her students use language as a bridge into another, more comfortable America.

Had the corps members not been there, other teachers would have stood in their places. But they would not have been as well educated. And they would in all likelihood not have been better prepared.

Since the summer of 1990, Teach for America has gone on to recruit, train and place another over two thousand teachers. It has mushroomed into a multi-million dollar organization that has reached tens of thousands of American school children. And it only keeps growing. The program continues to attract funding, attention and thousands of applicants from the nation's top universities.

But the corps members' moments of success present a challenge — for Teach for America, for the educational establishment, for the schools of education: All the talk of educational reform, all the proposals for school choice, for decentralized administrations, for new curricula or a return to basics, all of them are meaningless without good teachers. And there are too few good teachers in this country.

The lesson of Teach for America, the lesson that the corps members took with them from the classroom, is that there is more, far more to teaching than simply being smart and idealistic.

A good teacher can change lives. And yet we do a great injustice to teachers sent unprepared into the classroom. Teach for America has gotten a generation thinking about teaching. But now it is time to create a generation of real teachers — teachers who think of themselves as bright, prepared, respected professionals.

Teach for America has succeeded. But it has done so by default. For all the criticism of the program's approach — the hasty training followed by parachuting into classrooms — the sad fact is that, systematically, there are no better alternatives to getting desirable people into undesirable schools.

There are, of course, the occasional gifted teachers and visionary administrators who have not necessarily graduated from Ivy League schools. But their stories are so rare and their successes so uncommon that they become the subjects of movies, books and newspaper profiles, the one-in-a-million story of the teacher who triumphed. But celebrating heroes further condemns the system they fight, for the bouquets are another way of saying, Look what it takes to endure there. What those stories are also saying, of course, is that you can.

That is what Teach for America is saying, too. The program based its existence on the simple and disturbing premise that what we have does not work.

But is Teach for America the answer? Yes, and no. The success of Teach for America is rooted, in good measure, upon its speed. It has quickly succeeded in making teaching so attractive a choice — if only for two years — that five college graduates who might not have considered teaching are applying for every place in the program. So, too, has Teach for America succeeded in getting those people into the classroom, filling a chronic shortage in the nation's most beleaguered schools. It has quickly learned from its early mistakes — and is now providing the kinds of support, through mentors and outside counselors, that the first group of corps members lacked. That people who have many career choices are, if only temporarily, choosing teaching, cannot help but enhance the standing of the profession.

But there are dangers in Teach for America's success. There is a danger, first, not in the program but in the way it is perceived — in the idea that there exists, at least in part, an easy and inexpensive answer to the problems that beset American education. What the corps members learned, of course, is how inapplicable the word "easy" is to any aspect of schooling. They learned how hard it is to control a group of students, to engage them and make them want to learn, while at the same time satisfying arbitrary bureaucratic demands. On a larger scale, they learned how difficult it is to reform a system that no longer serves to produce the best students, but which contents itself with a range of achievement from failure to mediocrity.

There is a danger, too, in thinking that the Teach for America formula for preparing teachers is widely applicable. It works because it ensures a quick path to the classroom for people who are not necessarily inclined toward a year's internship, but who want students of their own now.

The corps members would, in all likelihood, have been better served by spending their first year in school assisting, and learning from, an experienced teacher, while taking courses on such subjects as how children learn and how best to teach them. But that is not going to happen with the people whom Teach for America is recruiting. Still, if the program's rapid, and subsequent on-the-job training did these new teachers, and their students few favors, neither did most schools of education.

Criticisms of its approach aside, Teach for America's successes, like the success of the Teacher Corps before it, speak of the possibilities of a streamlined, professional teacher preparation program. You do not necessarily need four years to make a teacher. What has become ever more apparent is that what works is an approach similar to other professional training programs, be it law, medicine, or journalism. The most innovative teacher education programs combine classroom internships with course work — course work that not only teaches theory but which explains and examines the real life lessons of those classrooms.

To her credit, Wendy Kopp is looking beyond the immediate aims of her program to new ways of recruiting and training teachers. In an article in the *Yale Law & Policy Review* titled "Reforming Schools of Education Will Not Be Enough" she argued that school districts should be responsible for finding and preparing their own teachers. The cost of preparing these teachers would be the district's, which could either do the training itself or contract out the work. And like Teach for America, the districts should seek out the best people and not just assume that a person who has many career options would not be interested in teaching.

It is one thing, however, to recruit people for a limited commitment, even, as Teach for America envisions, people who will become advocates for public education wherever they go. It is, at this point, still quite another to get good people to stay. Even those corps members who were staying on said they'd do so for perhaps another year or two. They had seen enough to convince them that they did not want to grow old as teachers.

And the best of them will not stay in any great numbers until they are accorded the respect and dignity that we all say teachers are due, but which we too seldom extend. What the corps members learned is that school remains a place where respect is an elusive quality. Teachers do not respect students and students, administrators and parents too often do not respect teachers. The result is schools that drift along, hour to hour, day to day, month to month, with little passion, little joy and little asked other than a safe and quiet completion of the term.

For all that Teach for America was accomplishing in raising the standing of the profession on campuses across the country, the real work of transforming teaching — and with it, beginning to transform schools on the most basic level of the classroom — is not just in getting people with impressive resumes into schools. It is still about making people see schools as a stimulating workplace, not a dungeon.

And that will not happen until the way we look at school, and what we demand of schools, changes. Nothing changes until the day teachers earn as much as school janitors and are given a voice in creating their schools, until parents stop cringing and offering thin smiles of feigned pleasure when their children tell them they are considering teaching. Nothing changes until schools teach children the way they really learn, and until schools help children see a connection between those lessons and their lives.

These changes are not about making school easier, but more challenging, for students and their teachers. Because by raising the stakes, by saying, You are capable of these things, schools say to children and their teachers that they are worthy of being entrusted with finding their own ways to mastery and excellence.

Good people, smart and committed people, get excited when they are working in schools with missions, schools where the goal is not merely making sure children leave school knowing things, but also helping them become learners. Virtually all children are capable of learning, in their own way and at their own pace, the lessons they will need at the various stages of their lives. And they are capable, and eager, too, to continue the process of learning they carried with them into the classroom, and which is too often squelched in the interests of "teaching."

Can Teach for America make a difference beyond its present, narrow scope? Yes, to a degree. By doing as the Teacher Corps did before it, Teach for America gives its teachers chances to come together, not just to gripe, but to compare notes about what worked and what didn't. From such gatherings come the sense that they are not in this alone, that there are other teachers across town, across the state and across the country who are doing and thinking the same things. There are few feelings quite as uplifting as being are part of something larger, a movement, a cause. If Teach for America can galvanize its corps members, and perhaps bring other teachers along with them, it can create a powerful force for reform. Because unlike so many teachers whose schooling, training and work life only increase their sense of their own limitations, Teach for America works to recruit people who display that wonderful gift of being young and filled with belief in themselves. If as individuals they feel thwarted in their desire to do things differently, then perhaps as a group they will not.

I have heard my parents talk for years of the occasional arrival at their schools of someone young, inexperienced, bright and eager and how, in my mother's words, you have to tend that new teacher like a rare and delicate sapling. Because then that new teacher might actually make it, might not only survive his or her first two years in the classroom, but might become a teacher who stays and flourishes.

What they need, beyond encouragement and hand holding and ongoing instruction, are reminders of hope. Because like the corps members these new teachers have all learned that hope exists in school, even in the least likely places. Hope endures because in the end children, no matter who they are, where they live, and what they experience, still want to know. And they will leap, if given a chance.

Teach for America offers scores of testimonials that confirm all that we have heard and read about the crises in the nation's classrooms — the crises of failure, indifference, and mediocrity. But those same testimonials also confirm that the very children we have come to dismiss as uneducable, who are remanded to schools to which most of us would never think of sending our own children, are just as eager as all the other children to learn. They sit all but abandoned, a resource we dismiss for their unfortunate circumstances.

Like their teachers, and like their own parents, these children are overwhelmed by forces that make them feel ever more hopeless. But even after years of being ground down by schools that offer them little but confirmation of their worst fears about themselves, they still show that, when given the right person and the right lesson and the right encouragement, the look in their eyes will turn from rage, indifference and confusion, to something altogether different: to the look of wonder and pleasure as the world opens before them.

Acknowledgments

THE IDEA FOR THIS BOOK was first proposed to me in the winter of 1990 by Thatcher Drew, who had produced the Emmy-nominated PBS documentary, "Who Will Teach for America?" from which this book draws its title. Thatcher was interested in going beyond the scope of the documentary, and exploring in the greater depth and detail that a book allows, the idea of what a new corps of teachers could mean for the children in some of America's most troubled classrooms. The idea was to use the same teachers who had been featured in the documentary, and then to explore the larger educational and social issues at play in their experiences in the classroom.

I am indebted to Thatcher for that idea, but most especially for his faith in this book. It was an idea he simply would not let die. I am also indebted to Doc Jarden, who produced and directed the documentary, for his encouragement and help.

I want to thank The Merck Company Foundation and Connecticut Public Television for their support in this project. Merck was also a major backer of the original documentary and offered its assistance without condition and review.

My thanks to Ho Chang, Jill Gaulding, Vicki McGhee, Miguel Ceballos, Tom Super, Jane Martinez and Julie Burstein, for their time and cooperation — enduring a whole new round of questions just when they thought they were done. My thanks, too, to Roy Campbell of Teachers

College, and Dudley Blodgett at the Harvard Graduate School of Education for putting me in touch with many of the educational thinkers and reformers whose names and ideas appear in the book. Ann Cook was invaluable in introducing me to the world of the alternative high school.

Susanna Rodell read the manuscript and offered her sound ideas as well as her encouragement. Peter Coveney's editing was incisive and invaluable. My agent, Barney Karpfinger, proved, once again, how lucky a writer can be when he has a wise and thoughtful agent in his corner.

I was indeed fortunate to be able to avail myself of two vetting services. My parents, Herbert and Lorraine Shapiro, have been educators for over 40 years. They have never tired of the task and have never stopped thinking of ways of doing it better. Time and again I was able to call upon them to explain what they had encountered in the classroom, and to put in perspective the stories I was hearing from this group of fledgling teachers. And then there was my wife, Susan Chira, who is a National Education Correspondent for *The New York Times*. Not only did she read the manuscript with a sense of what was taking place in schools across the nation, but was invaluable in helping me refine and articulate the ideas that emerged in the book. It is her faith and support for which I am most grateful of all.

Selected Bibliography

Clifford, Geraldine Joncich and Guthrie, James W. *Ed School.* Chicago: University of Chicago, 1990.

Comer, James P. *Maggie's American Dream: The Life and Times of a Black Family.* New York: Plume/NAL, 1980.

——. *School Power: Implications of an Intervention Project.* New York: Free Press, 1980.

Crawford, James. *Bilingual Education: History, Politics, Theory and Practice.* Trenton, New Jersey: Crane, 1989.

Duschl, Richard A. *Restructuring Science Education: The Importance of Theories and Their Development.* New York: Teachers College, 1990.

Finn, Chester E., Jr. *We Must Take Charge: The Schools and Our Future.* New York: Free Press, 1991.

Fiske, Edward B. *Smart Schools, Smart Kids: Why Do Some Schools Work?* New York: Simon & Schuster, 1991.

Freedman, Samuel G. *Small Victories: The Real World of a Teacher, Her Students, & Their High School.* New York: Harper & Row, 1990.

Gardner, Howard. *The Unschooled Mind: How Children Think and How Schools Should Teach.* New York: Basic Books, 1991.

Johnson, Susan Moore. *Teachers At Work: Achieving Success in Our Schools.* New York: Basic Books, 1990.

Kane, Pearl Rock. ed. *The First Year of Teaching: Real World Stories from America's Teachers.* New York: Walker, 1991.

Kobrin, David. *In There With the Kids: Teaching in Today's Classrooms.* Boston: Houghton Mifflin, 1992.

Kozol, Jonathan. *Savage Inequalities: Children in America's Schools.* New York: Crown, 1991.

Mithaug, Dennis E. *Self-Determined Kids: Helping Children Succeed.* New York: Free Press, 1991.

Silberman, Arlene. *Growing Up Writing: Teaching Children to Write, Think, and Learn.* New York: Times Books, 1989.

Sizer, Theodore R. *Horace's Compromise: The Dilemma of the American High School.* Boston: Houghton Mifflin, 1985.

———. *Horace's School: Redesigning the American High School.* Boston: Houghton Mifflin, 1992.

About the Author

MICHAEL SHAPIRO is the author of *Japan: In the Land of the Brokenhearted* (New York: Henry Holt, 1989) and *The Shadow in the Sun; A Korean Year of Love and Sorrow* (New York: Atlantic Monthly Press, 1990). His work appears in such publications as *The New York Times Magazine, Esquire, The Village Voice, Sports Illustrated, Mirabella, World Monitor,* and *GQ.* He is an assistant professor at the Columbia University Graduate School of Journalism. He lives in New York with his wife, Susan Chira, and their daughter, Eliza.